The Retirement Challenge

A Non-Financial Guide From Top Retirement Experts

Retirement Coaches Association

Table of Contents

Introduction

There I was, sitting alone in a hotel lobby when an odd email popped up.

It read: "Great article, where can I learn more about your association?"

I was initially caught off guard, thinking, "What article and association is he talking about?"

Then, I quickly remembered that a few weeks back a journalist reached out to me with some questions about retirement coaching. It was a writer who worked for a number of media outlets, so when I replied to his inquiry, I didn't even ask which paper it was for. I was just happy to get quoted.

So, I went to the internet to see if I could find the article. And that's when complete and total panic set in.

The article took up half of a page in *USA Today* and said I was "spearheading the Retirement Coaches Association."

That was 100% true, the only problem was, we were still in the initial planning stages. Quite frankly, I hadn't even secured a domain name for the group yet.

As the emails, comments, and requests for more information came in over the subsequent days and weeks, I knew we were on to something big. Seven days later, we had an initial website and the RCA not only became a reality, but has blossomed into something more remarkable than I ever imagined.

The caliber of people who were called to this industry is impressive. I have never been around a group of professionals who are more credentialed, experienced, and committed to changing the retirement planning process ever before.

As I got to know all of the members and their respective areas of expertise, the next big opportunity for the RCA showed up: Putting all of our knowledge and experience into one place in order to have a bigger impact on the individuals, couples, groups and communities we serve.

When I initially put the call out to members who would be interested in contributing a chapter, I expected 10-12 people to respond and for a few of those people to potentially fall off for one reason or another. I was pleasantly surprised when more than 20 people raised their hands, including several who wanted to contribute multiple chapters.

As a result, we had 24 different members contribute 26 insightful chapters, covering nearly every aspect of retirement you could imagine. It's the first book of its kind and does something that is missing from mainstream articles and discussions in this area.

It digs deep and delivers powerful content that:

- Takes readers on a personal journey to help them thrive in their transition

- Offers a new sense of purpose for those who are unsure of, or conflicted by retirement decision

- Provides peace of mind by acknowledging you're not alone no matter what you may be dealing with

- Validates what you may have been thinking about while providing direction for your situation

- Allows you to see the beauty and benefits of planning beyond the dollars and cents of retirement

In the end, we are the Retirement Coaches Association! A group of committed professionals who are here to make an impact and help you thrive in your transition from work life to home life. In each chapter, you will not only have the opportunity to learn and expand your thoughts about retirement, but also learn more about each member. Please don't hesitate to share your direct thoughts and feedback with the authors who made a difference for you.

Sincerely,

Robert Laura

Founder, Retirement Coaches Association

www.RetirementCoachesAssociation.org

Your Mindset Matters

By Marianne Oehser

Your Mindset Matters

What is mindset anyway? It is the attitudes and beliefs you hold. It is not all the beliefs and attitudes you have — just the ones that help you sort out what is happening in your life and orient you as you handle the situations you encounter.

Why Mindset Matters

Your mindset can allow you to see the possibilities ahead or keep you stuck in unproductive ways of thinking.

After decades of research, world-renowned Stanford University psychologist Carol S. Dweck, PhD, discovered a simple but important idea: the power of mindset. In her book, *Mindset: The New Psychology of Success*, she shows how success in almost every area of human endeavor can be dramatically influenced by how we think about our talents and abilities.

She says that there are people with a *fixed mindset* and those with a *growth mindset* about where their abilities come from.

- Someone with a fixed mindset believes that their ability is innate and can't be changed. A failure makes them doubt how good they are. People with this mindset feel that they have to prove themselves and they get very defensive when someone suggests they made a mistake.

- Someone with a growth mindset believes they can improve their ability. Failure shows them what they need to work on. They often show perseverance and resilience when they make a mistake and become motivated to work harder.

One of the most powerful aspects of mindsets is that they can be shifted quickly. Unlike skills that have to be practiced over and over, mindsets sometimes shift dramatically. In her book, Dr. Dweck tells the story of a young man named Jimmy. He was a junior high student who had very little interest in his classes. One day he sat through a class describing the growth mindset. At the end of the presentation, he tearfully asked, "You mean I don't have to be dumb?" From that point on, Jimmy became a hard-working student. His mindset had been that he was dumb so why bother studying. Once he shifted his belief and was open to the possibility that maybe he really wasn't dumb, he began to think that maybe he could get good grades and started working on making that happen.

The Stories We Tell Ourselves

> "The most important story you will ever tell about yourself is the story you tell _to_ yourself."
>
> — Jim Loehr, author of The Power of Story

Telling stories is fundamental to who we are as human beings. Stories are older than the written word and exist in every culture. They were told around the campfire before there were books and as you put your children to bed. They entertain and teach important lessons.

The stories we tell <u>ourselves</u> are the way we interpret our experiences and make sense out of life. They are so much a part of us that they determine how we respond to situations and other people. Our stories shape how we perceive the world and motivate the choices we make. We even use them to make sense of who we are as human beings. Yet, they are largely unconscious. Most of the time we are not even aware of them.

The problem with the stories we tell ourselves is sometimes they are not really the truth and we often get attached to ones that do not serve us.

This old tale illustrates this.

Cracked Pot Story

A water bearer in India had two large pots, each hung on each end of a pole that he carried across his back.

One of the pots had a crack in it and the other pot was perfect. The perfect one always delivered a full portion of water at the end of the long walk from the stream to the master's house. The cracked pot arrived only half full.

For two years this went on daily, with the bearer delivering only one and a half pots of water to his master's house.

Of course, the perfect pot was proud of its accomplishments.

But the poor cracked pot was ashamed of its imperfection. It was miserable that it was able to accomplish only half of what it had been made to do.

After two years of what it perceived to be a bitter failure, it finally said to the water bearer,
"I am ashamed of myself, and I want to apologize."

"Why?" asked the water bearer.

"For the past two years, I've delivered only half my load because of the crack in my side.
Because of my flaws, you have to do more work."

The water bearer felt sorry for the old cracked pot, and said, "As we return to the master's house, I want you to notice the beautiful flowers along the path."

As they went up the hill, the old cracked pot saw the beautiful wildflowers on the side of the path.
But, it still felt bad because it had leaked out half its load.

The bearer said to the pot, "Did you notice that there were flowers only on your side of your path, but not on the other pot's side? That's because I've always known about your flaw, and I took advantage of it.

I planted flower seeds on your side of the path, and every day while we walk back from the stream, you've been watering them. For two years I have been able to pick these beautiful flowers to decorate my master's table.

Without you being just the way you are, we would not all have this beauty."

— Author unknown

The moral of the story is that each of us has our own unique flaws. We are all cracked pots. Are you telling yourself a story like the cracked pot did that you are limited and not as good as someone else? Perhaps a better story would be about the possibilities you have in front of you.

Do you know what stories you are telling yourself about who you are or the circumstances in your life?

Most of the time our stories are running like background music and we are not really aware of them. We will never stop telling ourselves stories about those things — that is just how we are made. Becoming aware of your stories and what you are believing is an important step to being in control of your behavior. That means you have to tune into the background music.

- Let's start with identifying the positive stories. The ones that are resulting in things going the way you want them to go. Think about the areas of your life that are going well. Step back and look at what you believe about yourself or the situation.

- The negative stories are often a bit harder to get in touch with. What area of your life is not going as well as you would like? What is the story you are telling yourself here?

- Write the story down. Writing it forces you to see it more clearly. Be as honest and specific as you can be. No one will see what you write unless you decide to share it. Describe your thinking process, how you are feeling, and everything else that comes up for you. Try not to rationalize or blame anyone.

- Just like any good story, it will probably take a few drafts before you get it right. Put it aside for a day and when you go back to it try to embellish it more. You'll know when you have it right.

Then, ask yourself if your story is serving you now. Is it true today? Like the Cracked Pot, is there another way to look at it? Is your story allowing you to see the possibilities ahead or is it keeping you stuck in unproductive thinking?

At this point, you have a choice. Do you want to continue using that story or like Jimmy, the junior high school student, do you want to rewrite it? You are the author so you can write your new story any way you want to.

What's Your Mindset About Retirement

Do you look at retirement with euphoria or a sense of doom and gloom?

The Euphoric View

As we approach retirement, most of us are ready to say goodbye to the hectic pace and all the stress that goes with most careers. We are ready to downshift a bit and are excited about enjoying our much earned 'vacation.' The retirement picture we create in our minds is often the Hollywood version with lots of excitement but not much clarity. It's filled with images of things we want to do – travel, golf, tennis, boating, or anything else we have dreamed of doing. And, for many of us, that is just how retirement starts. There really is a retirement honeymoon and it feels pretty euphoric.

Just like any honeymoon, it is not a permanent state. It is simply not realistic to expect the euphoria and the newness to last forever — but somehow, we do it anyway. We think that being on vacation for 20 years will continue to have the same excitement that it had in the beginning. But, it doesn't — it fades. As one of my clients once said, "We've checked off most the things on our bucket list and we still have a good 20 more years ahead. What do we do now?"

When your expectation is that retirement will always have the thrill of being on vacation that you felt when you were escaping the pressures of your career, you will be disappointed. The day will come when all the play is not as much fun as it was in the beginning.

I was talking to one of my former colleagues about a year after she retired. She is an excellent golfer and had planned to play golf at least five days a week when she retired. She even toyed with turning pro. When she called, her retirement honeymoon was ending and she was no longer enjoying playing golf so often. She said, "Some days I'm euphoric that I am retired and other days I think I made a terrible mistake."

This can create a new kind of stress. Retirement no longer fits your Hollywood image and you don't know what to do about it. You are no longer sure what you want your days and weeks to be like. You probably feel like you are a bit adrift.

That is when it's time to get serious about building your Happiness Portfolio®. That means designing your new life so that it is balanced and diversified just like your financial portfolio. Research shows that the people who are the happiest in retirement are those who invest time and energy in all aspects of their life: having fulfilling relationships, enjoying social connections, making a contribution in some way, maintaining your health, enjoying leisure activities, growing as a human being in some way, and incorporating spirituality — whatever that means to you.

The Gloom-and-Doom View

The opposite of the euphoric mindset is the gloom-and-doom mindset. The gloom-and-doom mindset looks at retirement as the end of the line. The story it tells you is that all the good things in your life are over and there is nothing more to look forward to. It tells you that you are being put out to pasture because you are useless. It says that everything is downhill from here and focuses on your own mortality.

One of the big problems with such a negative outlook on this chapter of your life is that it can become a self-fulfilling prophecy. When you are focused on all of the things that are potentially bad about this new phase, you are not likely to see the endless possibilities for how great your life can be now. This kind of thinking can negatively impact your health and lots of research studies have shown that it will. It will definitely turn you into a very grumpy person and can lead to serious depression.

Of course, there are some very legitimate things that are not so wonderful about this phase of our lives. You probably don't have the boundless energy of your youth. You might fear that you will become 'irrelevant' and may not keep up with all of the knowledge and technology changes that will certainly evolve. A whole segment of your social life will disappear — the people you interacted with as part of your career. These things are real but you don't have to let them take you down a rabbit hole you can't get out of.

Shifting your outlook to a more positive perspective will allow you to look at things differently. When you choose a story about what is ahead that includes the possibility that there are more positive things ahead, even much more good stuff ahead. That shift will allow you to see ways to deal with the downsides of life after your career.

Sometimes 'dealing' with something means accepting that it is and letting go of it. For example, if you were in a very technical field, you may have to acknowledge that you are no longer going to be the expert you once were and enjoy the fact that you were respected for that knowledge. *Or,* you may look for a new way to apply the knowledge you have. It may be as a hobby, in a volunteer role, or as a new encore career. Staying engaged with what you were good at might give you the incentive to stay up with the technology related to it.

Neither the euphoric nor the gloom-and-doom way of looking at retirement serve you very well in the long run.

Carl Jung, the Swiss psychologist and the founder of Analytical Psychology, offers us another way of looking at this stage of life. He talks about the "afternoon of life." The morning of our life is focused on achieving things — getting an education, building a career, raising a family, acquiring things, becoming someone. Dr. Jung says the "afternoon of life" is not just a "pitiful appendage to life's morning" and rather than seeing our afternoon as a process of reduction, he says it is a process of expansion.

"The afternoon of life is just as full of meaning as the morning; only, its meaning and purpose are different...."

— Carl G. Jung, PhD

This way of looking at the new chapter of your life suggests that there is much to be savored about it. The afternoon just has a different rhythm than the morning. It may be a time for slowing down a bit but it can still be filled with enthusiasm and activity. It is an opportunity to focus on different things than you did in the morning of your life. It is an opportunity to see new and different possibilities for how you invest your time and energy. It is a time to discover the meaning and purpose of your own afternoon.

It's time to bask in your afternoon sun.

About the Author

Marianne Oehser is a retirement consultant, Certified Retirement Coach, and founder of Retire & Be Happy. She is a seasoned expert committed to helping people create a happy, fulfilling "post-career" phase of their lives through her workshops, seminars, public speaking, and individual coaching. She also works with singles and couples to successfully build and maintain healthy and rewarding relationships — after all, having a solid relationship is central to creating a happy, fulfilling life. Marianne holds a Masters of Management from Northwestern University Kellogg School of Management.

11

Your Fears: How To Use Them To Your Advantage In Creating The Life Of Your Dreams

By Larry Jacobson

If I Can Do It, So Can You

In this chapter, you're going to learn how to overcome the biggest challenge to creating your dream retirement lifestyle: fear. Why should you listen to me? Because I speak from experience. After I retired from a 20-year career in the corporate world, I then spent six years sailing my own boat around the world and documented my process of letting go of my previous life.

I spent an entire year reverse-engineering the thoughts, challenges, and actions I experienced, and compared them to those of my current coaching clients. They matched, so I know just what you're feeling because we all go through a similar process. Now my passion is helping people like you redefine your retirement and follow your passions without letting fear get in the way.

I first stepped foot into a tiny sailboat at the age of 13 and was hooked. I found my passion and from that day on, I dreamed about achieving the Everest of sailing: captaining my own boat all the way around the world.

Nothing was going to stand in my way and, from Day 1 of this idea, I never doubted I would do it. I never hesitated to say, "I'm going to sail around the world."

I also never admitted that the idea scared the heck out of me.

It wasn't until 33 years later, I sailed out beneath the Golden Gate Bridge, turned south, and headed for places unknown. I proved once again the world is round: If you sail west far enough, you *do* end up back where you started.

After six years, 40,000 miles, and 40 countries, I sailed back triumphantly underneath the same bridge after completing a circumnavigation. Then, I wrote an award-winning memoir about it to encourage others to achieve their dreams. If I can do that, then you can overcome the fears I know many of you are experiencing.

I became an expert on fear — not out of desire, but from necessity — as I learned to live with it nearly every day for six years.

The End Of Your Script: A Blank Page Awaits Your Plan

Most of life's chapters are scripted and we follow an established progression from one stage to the next. In school, we advanced from kindergarten to elementary, from middle to high school, and the next step for some was college, the military, or civic service.

In the corporate world, you climb the ladder from supervisor to manager, director, vice president, president, and then the C-suite. If you're in the military, you similarly rise through the ranks in proper order.

But now that you're at an unscripted part of your life, living longer than expected, you have to — rather, you get to — write your own script for the rest of your years.

Yet, when many of us are finally given the chance to write our own script, we don't do it — because we're afraid. That presents a problem because, as they say on Broadway, "If it isn't on the page, it isn't on the stage." This chapter will help you get through your fears so you can write your script and begin living again.

What Are You Afraid Of? Risking What You Have

What are we afraid of that paralyzes or freezes us from moving forward? Before I answer that, first I want you to know that 70% of retirees don't have a plan for what to do with their time in retirement because they fear creating one. With 10,000 new retirees per day just in the U.S., you can be confident you're not alone.

Let's jump right in and identify what you might be afraid of. If you can define what you fear, you are much better prepared to deal with the fears. The first big fear of most retirees is not anything you don't have, it's what you do have. It's the good things in your life you're afraid of risking and losing.

I understand this concept very well. When I left to go sailing, I was risking much of the life I had built. I let go of my career, 20 years in the making and basically committed career suicide, never to return to my field of work.

My income stopped abruptly, going from pretty good to zero in a flash. I traded my secure comfort for a life of the unknown: I no longer had a car in the driveway, nor a local grocer who knew my name. I gave up my home for a life of adventure — not only my physical house, but I left my friends and family, not knowing when or if I would ever see any of them again.

And lastly, I gave up what retirees fear letting go more than anything: my identity. I let go of how I identified myself as a career executive for the past 20 years. Who was I going to become? It was terrifying. Sailing away was the scariest day of my life, the riskiest, and yet it was oddly thrilling at the same time.

It would have been easy to let circumstances decide for me, stay at home with my good secure life, and pass up a chance at my dream. Like me, you have these same good things in your life: career, income, security, home, identity, kids, dogs, cats, yoga on Thursdays, the grandkids' soccer on Saturdays, and church on Sundays.

All reasons not to take risks. It can be as simple as, "I've always wanted to move to Italy to write for a year, but who would watch the grandkids, and what about my cat?"

Whatever it is you want to do, there's going to be some sort of a risk. And we all know the rules: No risk, no reward, and usually the bigger the risk, the bigger the reward. So why not take the time to analyze the risks you will be taking to create your dream retirement by asking yourself some questions?

- What are you risking? How important is it to keep and how would losing it affect your life?

- What will be the worst thing to happen if you fail in your endeavors in a new direction? How do you measure failure, by trying? What if you positively affect one person, isn't that success?

- What will be the good that happens if you succeed and how do you measure success in your life?

While sailing around the world, I discovered that while achieving the ultimate goal of circumnavigation was important, the journey was truly the enjoyable part. So if your big dream is to start a nationwide clothing drive, and you end up clothing 10 homeless people — you change 10 lives — do you see that as success? I do.

Use Your Passion To Drive Through Fear

Still, with all those good things in your life, why take a risk that is scary, especially if it's self-imposed? How do you justify to yourself taking risks? Why not just be happy with what you have? Because your passion drives you to take risks. Not to worry though, as it's also your passions that will carry you through your fears.

Chances are you're not going to risk everything like I did, because you're not as crazy as I am, and don't care to sail around the world. For you and your dreams, the risks will be different.

For example: If you've always wanted to open a corner coffee shop, you'll want to be open on weekends. But if your grandkids have soccer on Saturday mornings and you like to attend church services on Sunday mornings, are you willing to risk giving up both of those events? If not, then you might want to reconsider and make it an afternoon tea shop.

Focus on your passion, not the risk. Stack the deck in your favor so you can give your plan a chance of succeeding. And remember your passion is worth the risk.

If you don't know what you're most passionate about, take the free passion quiz at www.larryjacobson.com/passion-quiz.

Fear of Losing Your Identity: Who Are You Now?

Every retiree I've coached fears losing their identity. I often hear, "I used to be somebody, my name was on the door, and now I'm not needed anymore." And they're right. You're not needed that badly anymore, and corporate America isn't doing a very good job of helping with the transition from career to retirement.

(Are you listening corporate America?) I don't think I can say it any more clearly than this: I suggest you get another identity.

Don't say, "I'm a retired dentist." Instead, leverage your past identity and say, "I mentor new dentists on building their practices." It's important to focus on now and the future, not the past. The past can help shape the future, but it doesn't have to define it.

Fear Of Not Having Enough Time

This is a common fear. Many retirees feel there's not enough time to do what they have dreamed of doing. Maybe you want to go back to school and get your master's degree, learn a new skill, do the traveling and exploring you dreamed about, and volunteer to make a difference in the world. However, you fear there isn't enough time to finish your degree or become an expert at a new skill.

My response is, yes you do have enough time! Did you know that Baby Boomers are living 10-30 years longer than their parents? I have a client who used to be an attorney, is now 84 years young, and just took a part time legal clerk job. She loves it because she's respected for her years of wisdom. She works part time, and still has plenty of time for her children. Another client is 68 and just enrolled in college to get his master's degree in business.

Even if you start a project and don't finish, I'll repeat that it's the journey, not necessarily the destination that counts. Enjoy going to art class without feeling you have to become the next famous artist and open your own gallery.

Enjoy traveling to Italy and spending a week in the countryside, even if you don't live there for an entire summer. Start writing your memoir one page at a time, and you'll be surprised at how quickly the pages add up. Remember, neither words nor worry affect outcome, only action does. Take a little action today and it will lead to more action tomorrow.

Fear Of Not Knowing How To Do Something

The next fear retirees experience is that of not knowing how to do what you dream of doing. Many fear that, without the skills needed to do something, they shouldn't begin.

Nonsense! If I had waited to know how to do everything necessary to sail around the world, I never would have left the dock. But many people fear they're not an expert, so they don't begin. I'm living proof that you don't have to be the expert in your field *to* pursue your passion. You become an expert *as* you pursue your passion. I'm not specially gifted or exceptionally brave. I was just a regular guy who wanted to go sailing and was driven by passion. I became an adventurer by default. Out there, you either become brave or you turn around. You learn as you go, and your passion will drive you through any fear you have about not being an expert.

Begin by reading books, taking classes, and then take the first step of action. You'll be amazed at how quickly you learn, and how much experience and wisdom you have from other areas of your life. Taking on new ideas, hobbies, and projects, are easier because of your hard-earned knowledge and wisdom.

Fear Of Not Having A Big And Bold Idea For Your Life

While your passion is probably not to a desire to sail around the world, passion is passion, and it doesn't matter where you apply it. So, while you may not relate to sailing around the world, you may be passionate about coaching your grandkids' soccer team.

Your passion could be your family, re-building cars, eating good foods and exercising, reviewing books, starting a clothing drive, mentoring kids, or mentoring entrepreneurs. It could be going back to work in a new career or going back to school.

It doesn't matter what your passion is, if it's important to you, then pursue it, because its every bit as important and valid to you as sailing around the world was to me. I have "cut the dock lines" of several sailors who wanted to sail around the world but could only take a few months off. They went anyway and are having a wonderful time sailing the coast of Mexico. They're quite happy even though they aren't going to circumnavigate.

Your idea of a happy retirement should not be judged by the size or intensity of the endeavors you choose, but rather by how they make you feel. If you like the idea, then it's valid.

Fear Of Not Knowing What You Want

Many retirees don't have any idea what they want to do with their time in retirement, often because there are too many choices. The more choices you have, the harder it is to choose any particular one. That's why Costco sells one of each item. Being overwhelmed makes it too difficult to choose, and often ends in no choice. And not choosing something is making a decision to do nothing.

Fear of choosing the wrong direction can be paralyzing. What if you don't like the path you choose? Does it matter if your choice isn't perfect? You'll get a lot more satisfaction and miles under your keel by moving in an imperfect direction than you will by sitting at the dock talking about going sailing.

If you get into something that doesn't suit you, get out. You can always adjust and change your route. Leave the dock, take a step in any direction, just do something. Untie your dock lines and go!

Fearing Commitment

What if you fear committing to a new direction in life? What if you just want to wander awhile and wait and see, to discover what comes your way? Great, go for it. But I caution you that the wait-and-see attitude can often extend much longer than you expected.

We are all subject to Newton's law: "A body in motion stays in motion. A body at rest stays at rest."

If you plunk yourself down in front of the television, chances are that's where you'll stay.

My suggestion would be to commit to just one thing. It could be going to the gym two times a week, walking every evening, reading a new book each week, or joining a new social group. Commit to something, no matter how small. Who knows where it will lead you?

Fear of Making Decisions

It's common to fear making a big decision. You may not be sure of which way to decide, but you have to decide anyway. Sometimes decisions have to be made without all of the information necessary to make the decision. And that can be scary.

Some decisions are easy and without great consequence, while others are difficult and life-changing. I was unprepared to sail around the world. All I had was a boat, a dream, and my passion. I had never navigated across a 3,000-mile ocean before, but I ignored my cold feet and went anyway — because I was willing to make a decision based on my passion. It was a scary decision and one I had to make on my own. I didn't have all the information necessary, but the time came when I had to decide to go or not. Rather than listen to my fears and the naysayers ("Larry, you're gonna die out there!"), I listened to my passion. I recognized and accepted I was afraid and decided to go anyway.

It's a funny thing — in making scary decisions like leaving to cross an ocean or starting a new direction in life, you expect some sort of fanfare, a marching band, trumpets blaring. ("Hey! Look at me! I just made this really big decision!") But it doesn't happen that way.

No matter how long we wait, that marching band never seems to show up. And sometimes we keep waiting. Are you still waiting for your marching band to blare the fears away?

Are you stalling on an idea because there are no trumpets? And remember, making no decision *is* a decision. Taking no action *is* action. If you want something to happen, *you* have to make it happen.

How To Use Fear To Your Advantage

Now you know what fears to expect when planning your retirement lifestyle. So, what do you do about it? How do you manage these fears? This is an area I'm very familiar with. I lived with fear nearly every day for six years and I learned a lot about fear.

- Fear is nature's way of making you focus on the task at hand

- It sharpens your senses and makes you more alert

- You can use that fear and the additional sharpness to your advantage right there when you need it

Using fear to your advantage involves just two steps. Step 1 to using fear to your advantage is pretty easy: All you have to do is recognize the fear and admit you're afraid. You know what fear looks like. Your palms sweat, your eyes dart around taking in the situation, your heart beats faster, and your adrenalin is pumping.

Your vision becomes clearer, your muscles stronger, and you have boundless energy. You know what I mean — you've been there before.

Think back to a scary moment in your life — do you recognize the signs of fear? These are merely physiological reactions to fear to help in your natural fight or flight mode. This is your body taking care of itself, you're not having a heart attack!

Step 2 to using fear to your advantage is a bit trickier: After recognizing the fear, accept and embrace it. Accept that you are afraid. Know what it's doing *for* you. It's making you focused, sharper, and more alert. Those strengths can be used to your advantage to help get you through any situation.

When you embrace your fear, you disable it. You take away its power. Your fear is like the little red devil that sits on your shoulder telling you to do all those bad things like eat ice cream and have that third cocktail. This little fear devil can come along for the ride, but he no longer has any say in what you do or how you act.

Disarming Fear By Predicting It

By predicting fear is coming, you are better prepared to deal with it. When you are expecting to be afraid, you get a head start on recognizing and accepting the fear. When it arrives, you're ready for it, and can more easily use it to your advantage.

Of course, you may fear other elements of your retirement, and perhaps you don't share all the fears pointed out here. But I hope this chapter has helped you realize how you can take fear as an issue off the table.

Don't let fear stand in your way. Let the passion for your dreams guide you through your fears. Have confidence in your passion as a tool of strength. I wish you smooth fearless sailing.

Don't Let Fear Stop You From Achieving Your Goals

Exercises: Part I

Answering these questions will help solidify your knowledge of how to manage your fears.

1. What is one fear you are expecting to face that you may not have thought of yet? By identifying it now, you won't be surprised when it shows up!

2. You can follow this same exercise for as many expected fears as you like. The important part here is to learn the process. List some other fears you can expect.

3. To make your vision a reality and achieve the goals in your plan, you'll need to overcome the

fear of leaving the old and the familiar. What specifically are you afraid of leaving behind?

4. Beginning something new, and not yet being familiar with it, can be scary. Jot down something which is going to be part of your plan, but you don't' know how to do yet. Remember, the joy is in the journey and the learning.

5. You're going to be making a new plan — one you've never written before and this can be scary. Are you afraid of writing this plan? Why? You've written plans before and you can write this one too.

6. Without action, a plan is just a piece of paper. Fear often prevents us from taking the first step, but once you begin taking action, the rest will follow. Can you identify the first step in your plan and decide when you will take that first step?

Exercises: Part II

Now you're going to identify one of your biggest fears about moving forward with your goals and vision. After examining it closely, you'll see the fear truly is False Expectations Appearing Real.

You can follow this same exercise for as many fears as you like. The important part here is to learn and apply the process. I provide an example of a fear I had about crossing oceans. Notice how I broke it down to its elements. Try it with a fear of yours!

1. First, what is a big fear weighing on you?

   a. Example: Fear of crossing oceans

2. Now examine the fear closely and identify three elements that cause you to feel this fear.

   a. Run into storms

   b. Run out of food

   c. Be lost

3. Next, what are the pragmatic counter-arguments to the three elements above? What are the logical explanations why these elements aren't as valid as you originally thought?

   a. With skill and practice, you can see storms coming from hundreds of miles away.

   b. We carried a 3-month supply of food and caught enough fish to supplement our diet

   c. Skill and practice, plus today's modern navigation system, make it hard to get lost at sea

You should now be able to see your fears do not hold as much weight as you thought, nor are they as valid. You're free to move forward! Untie those dock lines and go!

About The Author

Larry Jacobson is nationally recognized in the field of non-fiscal retirement planning. His personal coaching and online video classroom were developed by reverse engineering his own experience. As speaker and retirement planning coach, he focuses on his groundbreaking program, Sail Into Retirement making retirement coaching accessible to more people. A California native, circumnavigator and adventurer, Jacobson is an avid sailor with over 50,000 blue water miles under his keel. Author of the six-time award-winning memoir of his six-year circumnavigation, The Boy Behind the Gate, he lives in the San Francisco Bay Area and welcomes new friends and inquiries at: http://larryjacobson.com/

The Right Work Can Keep You Young!

By Phyllis Horner, PhD

Envision the Benefits of Working Late

Let's start with a small request. Don't worry if it seems silly — it has a practical point.

Close your eyes and feel your current power, your energy, and your sense of meaning in life. Feel that for a minute. Now, with your eyes still closed, see a beautiful door ahead. The door is closed, and on the other side is the life you will live when you stop "working." Turn the knob, walk through the door and imagine yourself there. What kind of benefits do you feel? Imagine your energy, your power and meaning in life. What kind of losses might you experience?

If you're like many professionals who worked as employees, you feel free, alive, and self-directed for the first time in a long time. That's the good news. At the very same time, you may feel aimless, diminished, and retracted from the rhythm of vibrancy and the fast-moving stream of life — people describe it as more of a dispassionate observation of things happening. That's the downside.

Isn't it interesting that, once free of structure and direction from others, finally having enough time to contemplate what is really important in life, that time we have been longing for while "working for the weekend," that we can palpably feel a sense of loss?

What is that predicted loss for you? It's a vital question to consider.

The end of work is a reality for all people at some point in life, right? Yes, one day there will be no more work for each of us, no more external growth, though maybe spiritual growth occurs up till our last breath.

It's that space of external growth that I want you to consider for a while. Consider you are watching a documentary of a person who helped launch rockets, cure cancer, prevent catastrophe, or help another person learn a new skill.

Or, imagine the feeling if you are person who is doing one of those things, or one of thousands of other examples of positive action in our world.

In the imagined documentary, the person turns 66 years old, and just abruptly quits. What? That seems ridiculous, right in the middle of an important discovery or cause! But it's just what has been drummed into our heads as a norm, an expectation, and a right.

Some of us think, "Well, certainly I am not doing anything that others could not carry on without me," and then justify quitting, because leaving work with no meaning is OK.

Yes, of course that is true! It's also true that you have the right to stop working any time you want or need to, especially after this arbitrary age of 65. But here's a secret. Leaving work with little meaning or growth does not have to mean you stop working in your 60s. In fact, it's smart to look at what kind of work would bring real meaning and growth to you, in your own way, at this point in your life. Finding a way to self-determine your legacy and gifts to the current problems of the world and the next generations to follow is essential and it can bring youthfulness, and extended prosperity.

Another bonus, that most people don't realize, exists — it's an effect that has been experienced by others who gain an inheritance or otherwise no longer "need to work." The bonus is that the ogre of competition goes away. No longer do you need to be "better than," "as good as," or "good enough," to keep your role! Imagine what work would have been like all these years without that yoke of false judgment of worth attached to your effort.

In your mid-60s and beyond, any work you do comes with that freedom as well. The idea is that rather than fall into a decision to stop, you can make an active choice to consider what it could look like to be engaged in pursuits for a fee, at some level, for some amount of time.

Considered in this way, with full and free choice, you can make the search for work that "works for you" in late career a joyous one.

Many people across the United States share a growing interest in working during late career. Over half the population of working adults want to work longer than full retirement age. Is this right for you?

How should you think about it? What are your personal pros and cons? Let's take a look.

The What And Why Of Late Careers

What is a late career pathway? After doing extensive research and coaching of those entering this period in life, I've developed this working definition. "A late career pathway is paid work that you can do at your own pace. You choose your preferred environment, with your chosen schedule, and number of hours. You work with the type of people you want to be around. You use your natural talents and interests for a purpose you value. And, you work for a few years or many years, whether you are fully healthy physically or not."

How does that sound to you? Impossible? Good, if you need to work? Great, sign me up? Or are you thinking, "Hey, I'm not interested. I have my eye on that lounge chair with a tall drink at dusk." It's true that late careers excite some of us and bore others. This chapter helps you sort out your feelings about whether you can or should try a late career. And, it makes the case even if you have no plans to work later, that you should still, before you completely leave the world of work, create a blue-sky late career pathway, in case you change your mind. And, a lot of people do change their minds.

Here's a true story to illustrate. Joe was in sales all his life, first as a sales person for industrial equipment, then manager, and eventually director of his region. He was naturally outgoing and got bored easily, so when he moved to management and had to deal with processes and supervision, along with customer complaints and a routine schedule, he just hated it. By 55 he was disengaged. The problem was, he made too much money to quit and find something that paid as much. Like many of us, he traded meaning for material success.

By the time he was 60, he just couldn't wait to retire and he told his friends, "I'm outta here at 62. I can't wait to never think about work again!" True to his word, Joe retired at 62 and took Social Security. For a while, things were great. He relaxed, learned tennis, and traveled. But eventually, after about two years, he realized that his friends who were still working and he were drifting apart. He found himself lonely and out of touch. He lived alone, having divorced years before.

Joe was lucky, though. A friend told him about a freelance sales position in a related field. He took a contract and was elated, again for a while. This lasted 2 years before boredom arrived and he retired again. The last I heard, Joe had just started a new blog for sales using relationship selling. He's traveling, meeting new people, and making enough to support his travel.

Retirement is different for each person. That's the first message for you. Retirement also isn't just a one-time decision. It has potential to be much more complex, with many opportunities to decide what to do, if you start thinking and planning early.

How To Know Whether To Try A Late Career

Just like Joe, you will or have been faced with the palpable relief and joy that the parts of work you hate can be over. Just like him, you might see the freedom and the open road leading to your dreams of stress-free, happy days.

But before you begin to settle into that dream, I suggest you learn from Joe and start thinking earlier than he did. You see, Joe didn't think about some things that actually mattered a lot to him. He ignored his need to be around people to feel engaged in life. He didn't think about all his options. For example, he didn't realize there was a way he could go back to sales without standing up all day long. He was mainly escaping the pressure and monotony of management. He didn't plan — his escape parachute was not packed.

Consider that the question is not whether you should try a late career; it's whether you have a scenario where work could work for you later. First, you need to let yourself imagine, to "blue sky" what it could be, and then decide. You owe it to yourself. And, for this planning, the earlier, the better.

The Changing World of Work and Retirement

Today, as you likely know, there are many ways to successfully work. These include part-time, retainer, project work, freelance consulting, mentoring and coaching, online courses, and volunteering. Work can be for pay, for play or for barter. There's a detailed summary of the different options here. For now, here are four examples of people I know personally who are finding meaning and success, working in their late 70s and 80s.

Bill — having been a forester, a sales professional and a retiree for several years — is now an internet marketing professional who helps other late career people to set up websites and make money using affiliate links in an ethical way.

Carleen — a nationally known speaker and author — moved to Hawaii around retirement age because she loved the island life in her childhood. One of her sons lived there and owned a successful business so financially, there were no barriers. Carleen continued to work remotely, but at some point, she found herself needing renewal. She has now co-founded New Workforce Hawaii and is teaching people of all ages how to expand their ideas about how to work, and the value of self-directed work.

Jackie — a military wife who learned French cooking to create her own way in the world — later headed not-for-profit organizations and served in the local House of Representatives. She now serves on several local and national commissions including the role of women in the military, has finished a book, and will publish it later this year.

Doris — a long-time educator who retired with a broad network she kept building — now serves as interim leadership roles in colleges around the country.

These people are great role models of people who, though they don't have "encore careers" that take all their time, gain meaning and money from pursuits that also help the world. They have learned to pivot.

Pivoting

The broad variety of ways to work is great news for those of us who are just sick to death of the daily grind. Think of it! We can get rid of the parts of work that we can't stand anymore, and pivot to something more "like us." This idea of pivoting is a new career concept. In pivoting, to succeed, we switch out of a straight-line path and look at something from another angle. It's like going to the side door of your house instead of the front door, or moving from the seat you usually sit in to a different one, so that you gain a new perspective.

Here's a secret: Pivoting can keep you young. Pivoting stops us from looking at things through our old assumptions, our "old eyes", so to speak. It's refreshing and renewing to be open to be a beginner in thinking about things again.

Some Data

In my work with still-working clients who say they want to retire within 10 years, there is a lot of fear and trepidation about getting to retirement safely. Men worry that they will be bored with the life they have now and will be forced out of work before they are ready to go. Women worry that they will outlive their partner and their money, and will end up poor, stuck with relatives, or worse. No one, especially professional people who have become used to being valued in the world for what they know and who they are, wants to contemplate becoming dependent on others and losing control of their choices in life. No one wants to be invisible, unimportant, or "looked past" in conversations or at gatherings. Right? But if you do stop working, honestly, this is what happens.

How Late Career Pathways Help

For any person with 5-10 years left to retirement eligibility or more, early planning is the key to certainty and self-confidence about the future. The financial part of the planning is important, for sure. But planning for choices about work is equally important.

In the next section of this chapter, we will explore the five steps to this planning, which should be done alone and then with your partner in life, if there is one. Depending on your personality, it can take a few hours or a few weeks to get a couple of viable scenarios. People who don't like risk and who are more analytical, approach things differently than a person who likes the big picture buckets and chunks of data. This is normal and there is no one right way to approach things.

One important note — if you start your planning and your partner or spouse plans differently, it's important that each of you does it his or her own way — don't force one approach at the beginning. Why? Because things will "look good on paper" but one person isn't completely centered — they are conforming to the other person's viewpoint, and that's a big risk that will become evident later, after lifestyle decision that are hard to change are made.

Foundations of a Late Career Pathway: Meaning, Prosperity and Growth

Meaning

Quick, name the top few values of your life. Honesty? Family? Achievement? Service? What are they? Your meaning and the way you interpret any situation can be linked back to whether the event matches or is inconsistent with your core values. Whatever you will do next should actively support these values.

A lifestyle that is congruent with your values makes you feel happy, authentic, and lucky.

Prosperity

What makes you feel rich? How much money is sufficient to make you not pull in and feel constricted, miserly, resentful of those who are in need occasionally? How much does family harmony or a sense of having a life partner play into a feeling of prosperity? How about health?

Listing the top 3-4 aspects of prosperity in your ideal future centers you around the ability to be expansive and giving. It brings you what I call a "Holistic Richer Life".

Growth

What is your current definition of personal growth? Is it to learn a spiritual practice like yoga or chanting? To take up guitar or piano? To learn about healthy nutrition and exercise? To learn to build with wood or even 3D printers?

It is essential to know what is next from a growth standpoint. An analogy I like to use is the tree of life. The roots are your values. The prosperity is the fruit, the leaves, the harvest of your energy, purpose, and skills. The growth is at the edges of the tree, the new buds and shoots that guarantee the future is healthy and that the tree thrives.

What's the growth part of your tree of life going to look like? How does work play a role in that growth?

The Five Steps: How To Create Your Pathway

Remember that our definition of a Pathway is a plan for "still at work" that matches:

- The kind of work you would enjoy

- The kind of work the world values and needs

- The amount of time and energy you want to devote

- The amount of money you want to make to supplement your investments and savings

- The kind of people you like to be around, or who naturally value you

And, it's important that you only feel the need to commit to any possible work situation for 1-2 years at a time, so that you stay flexible and learn to pivot as life changes again. By the way, this is the secret to all successful career planning after 40 — even if you stay longer, don't assume you will.

Here's an example:

My colleague Debbie worked in university education for her whole career. She taught writing and literature, then moved into administration as chair of her department, and before she was eligible to retire with a full pension, was the chancellor for the satellite campus where she worked.

On the outside her situation looked good, but she was ready for something new — she had been working 40 years. On the inside, she still had a lot of mental energy and smarts. So, here's what Debbie did:

1. Kind of Work: She realized that she liked troubleshooting and problem-solving with other education professionals. She contacted through her network, peers in smaller colleges in another state where her son lived, a few years before her retirement date, and when she would visit him, she would also meet with and establish relationships with 3-4 of them.

2. Kind of Work in Demand: In her meetings with peers and by asking questions and observing the problems in the job she still had, she listed out 2-3 types of opportunities that might exist.

One was to serve as interim dean or the head of a department when the full-time person was on extended leave for medical reasons or sabbatical. The other was to serve in strategic or other special projects as the convener to solve future problems. For example, she studied how AI could impact campus enrollment and course offerings. Debbie started offering support informally when she could do so, even while she was still working.

3. Amount of Time and Energy to Devote: Debbie thought projects that took half time or less would be great, and not for the whole year. She had a lot of other interests and really wanted her life to change with retirement, not just be a "mini" of her former life. Once she "retired," to be sure her life changed, she moved to California in the same town as her son lived, so that she would get a real break.

4. Amount of Money: Debbie had a pension but also knew that she wanted to make enough money through work that it was "worth her time." She also decided that she wanted to make enough to not have to draw down her investments (beyond the minimum required), and she wanted a net positive cash flow for as long as she could get it.

5. Kind of People: Debbie liked to be around people with new ideas, who were interesting but not arrogant, who listened well, and who worked as a team, with little competition. So,

when evaluating possible opportunities, she spent a lot of time meeting the people she'd interact with.

Can you imagine your own answers to these questions? Even though this example may not be from your industry, the process works the same for lawyers, engineers, managers and executives, marketing and other experts, and anyone who has a talent the world needs less than full time.

Oh, and Debbie? She landed even more important roles than she had prior to "retiring," a result that surprised and pleased her immensely.

When To Plan

It's tempting to put planning off, when the need is not immediate. With all the "busyness of business" we have while fully employed at a job, we tend to act like we're a car in the fast lane on autopilot — we treat it like things will continue along the same path for as long as we want them to.

I think we do this because we are unsure of ourselves. Many of my clients, once they are in the planning process, feel so much better so fast that they wonder why they waited. And let's face it — it's not rocket science. In fact, this kind of planning is risk free and easy, the easiest future planning there is. The only real risk is not planning, and frankly, not getting past fear or exhaustion to open the door to an active future.

Some Realities

The case for having a plan to work late in life is clear and logical, but maybe you're still not convinced. Some recent statistics from Rand, a think tank, might be worth considering. In their American Working Conditions Survey released in 2017, they found that "unretirement is working for older Americans."[1]

- 40% of people over 50 were looking for a new job

- 39% of people in the workforce older than 65 had retired at least once and went back to work because of boredom or the need to be useful

My colleague Joseph adds this sobering truth: "This is the most important thing I noticed when I was retired for several years. Over time, I became unable to remember names or facts — I found myself searching for words or ways to express myself. This was alarming because I had always been an excellent communicator, and losing this ability made me feel old before my time, as well as worried that I would not be fully functional later. Luckily, once I returned to work, my abilities returned fairly easily. It's almost a 'use it or lose it' view of skills that we take for granted in our normal lives."

What's your next step? Who do you want to be 10 years from now? What do you want to know that you don't yet know? How do you want your legacy to proceed? What is the pathway to that legacy and purpose?

Consider work as a pathway, a predictable and useful method of ensuring you continually become who you can be, that your youthfulness continues indefinitely.

The journey to a late career pathway starts between your ears.

About The Author

Phyllis Horner, PhD, founder of Thriving Work Life Design and the Career Contentment by Design℠ Series, is a sought after mid-career and pre-retirement coach and work life success expert. She has positively affected the lives of thousands of people through her workshops, coaching and books. Based in Honolulu, Hawaii, she helps individuals, groups and couples across the US to find work that brings contentment, prosperity and meaning at any age. You can contact her at https://www.linkedin.com/in/phyllishorner, https://drphyllishorner.com, or by email at phyllis@thrivingworklife.com.

Notes

1. Nicole Maestas et al, *Working Conditions in the United States: Results of the 2015 American Working Conditions Survey* (Santa Monica, CA: RAND Corporation, 2017), https://www.rand.org/pubs/research_reports/RR2

Single, Retired, and Vulnerable

By Douglas Passanisi

It wasn't planned. It wasn't foreseen. In fact, I hadn't really thought about it, or ever internalized that I was already over 60, when "bam" — structural realignment, discontinuation of my position, and organizationally mandated retirement at age 62.

I had been working for a large, international, institution that was saying farewell to an entire level of management. The very institution that I had served night and day, protected and promoted, emailed and texted 24/7, secured donors for, and ensured the full engagement of its staff, terminated my position without warning.

Within three weeks, I had no office, no staff or budget to manage, and more importantly, no vision whatsoever of my future. I was 60, single, and "retired," feeling extremely vulnerable with no idea of what should or could be my next step.

Experiencing Loss

I joined the organization in my 40s, so had always been somewhat of a "late comer". Nonetheless, for nearly 20 years I worked as an international civil servant, traveled extensively, was chief of staff for over 100 staff members in eight locations globally, and made a good living. I bought a house and lived a comfortable, albeit extremely work-oriented, urban life.

During the subsequent weeks, before I actually left the organization, I went to see an experienced colleague who assured me that — with my experience and background — I would have no problem finding a host of interesting and lucrative jobs and opportunities. Filled with renewed confidence, I entered my first retirement.

As it turned out, my colleague was wrong. While she modified my CV, reiterated that ageism was a thing of the past, and was sure that similar jobs would be a quick win, she actually had no idea about the lack of demand for the international public service or for over-60 former civil servants.

While trying to embrace a new, online model for finding new work opportunities (including new job-search sites like Indeed), what I found was that I was overqualified, had too high a salary history, was competing with thousands of other (younger) candidates from all over the world, and was frankly unemployable in professional fields where I had years of relevant and unique experience. So what was I to do?

What I really felt was an extreme sense of loss. Work had always been the constant in my life from age 15. I gravitated towards positions of responsibility and problem-solving, and found fulfillment in the workplace which usually ended up being as much my home as my actual home.

A friend once noted that, for the amount of time I spent at my house, I maintained a rather expensive "place to sleep" since I left for work at 6 a.m. and returned at 10 p.m. I had always been, and enjoyed being, some form of a workaholic. The loss of work was thus much greater than I had ever imagined.

My income, my social network, my daily schedule, the engagement of my skills, my purpose — or rather my identity, all seemed to have ended along with my job.

What was most frustrating was that no one actually seemed to understand the extent of this loss. And even worse, friends — I mean, close friends — were unable to empathize with this dilemma or fully grasp that I needed to find a way out of what seemed to be a deepening hole. They just couldn't understand how *not* working was a bad thing. I mean, isn't that what we work for — not to work?

I even lost a few friends in the process because their suggestions were comments like, "Just go get a job," "What's the big deal?" "Enjoy not working," "So, you'll never work again?" "Go find something to do!" or "Well, if I were in your shoes, I'd be so happy."

They just didn't get how complex and profound retirement was. And — frankly — at first, neither did I. And when I did become aware of the magnitude of ending my career, it was ever so difficult to admit to anyone.

Healthy, Fit, and Vital At 60

What I noticed during those subsequent long hours at home was that I didn't have many friends over 60 or who had retired. And for those who had retired, the conditions for leaving work were quite different. The majority of my friends and colleagues were quite a bit younger than me. Some of my closest friends and work colleagues were some 10 and, in some cases, 20 years younger. And this became part of the challenge — recognizing that I had reached 60 without noticing.

I also had traveled since the age of 12 and friends and acquaintances were of various backgrounds, ages, and were culturally and linguistically diverse. So homogeneous relationships made me feel somewhat unchallenged and somehow uncomfortable. So, while I had been enjoying the ever-enlivening pleasure of being surrounded by energetic, diverse, and youthful friends, I honestly hadn't noted, deep down, that I had unintentionally entered the third act, the autumn years, the "over-the-hill gang".

This vision for my future was just not part of the way I had lived or envisioned my life. It was just not foreseen. But looking into the mirror, there was a fact that I had been ignoring— I was in my 60s, single, and now retired. It seemed overwhelming.

There are advantages and disadvantages to being single in retirement. You find yourself trying to display a youthful attitude in life and keep healthy and fit so you are ready for potential work challenges, maintaining productive energy levels, and frankly being attractive to potential new partners.

Being youthful or exuding youthfulness seems important when you're single. It makes one feel ready to engage and accessible to friends and colleagues. It also enhances confidence and vitality which are attractive attributes at any age.

While keeping fit and on your toes (anyone would like being noticed as having a youthful spirit or recognized as being a confident leader), there remains an aloneness, a vulnerability that can linger underneath, especially when you are single. And it is the recognition of this vulnerability that I found surfacing when I retired.

What I have learned in retirement is that a peer group of similarly experienced and retired individuals soon becomes nurturing and enlivening. You can seek out not only close friends in whom you can confide, but also retirees who face similar challenges, their own vulnerability, and the need for resilience.

What becomes evident with every passing year is that health concerns do, in fact, only increase as you age. As my physician says, "You know, when you reach a certain age…." When you do reach that certain age, and are single, health concerns are even a bit more concerning because there might not immediately be someone to check in with, to look at a bothersome bump, checkout a bald spot, confirm a broken tooth, or judge whether a doctor's visit is necessary.

Aching joints, coronary and respiratory changes, and an aging appearance, all increase with time. And, should you need basic over-50 checkups or procedures, there might not always be someone available to pick you up at the clinic, make a stop at the pharmacy, or prepare the chicken soup. You have to begin to intentionally plan these things a bit more carefully. Close friends, family, a health proxy, a person or persons who are not only present in your life but informed about your health issues, allergies, or doctors in case of emergency, becomes essential.

Parents and siblings also need to put in place a health plan because they too are aging and you might be called upon to care for a family member or make decisions regarding their health and well-being. Are you prepared to do that? I wasn't.

In my case, a family member, who had a limited health network, became terminally ill. While there was hospice care at home, day-to-day nursing care ended up being his siblings trying to figure out how best to care both during and after the illness. There were a whole set of unforeseen tasks with no real plans in place.

Discussing these issues with family members, *prior* to becoming too ill, is essential and becomes even more important with every year we grow older. It is not always an easy subject to approach. Physical well-being and living with zest and vitality goes hand-in-hand with the ability to talk about eventual health care, and yes, even death.

Does all this look dire? *Au contraire*. I am suggesting that as you transition to and through retirement, there are opportunities to continue to be fit and healthy, put all in order, get closer to friends and family by discussing our lives and legacies, embrace our relationships and support networks, and be less stressed and arbitrary and more at ease and intentional.

Taking Time Out for Leisure

What I discovered about myself in retirement was that I had not been especially engaged or challenged outside of work. I had never really focused on excelling at leisurely activities and frankly couldn't even define what leisure meant to me. I explored hobbies or interests to some extent but never fully internalized them for future engagement and fulfillment after work.

My sense of leisure was sitting at home alone in sweats with a cup of coffee responding to emails from work! Because my work phone was always on, so was I. I was so attuned to work that I hadn't fully invested in consciously building my own interests and passions for the future.

Taking out time to be quiet, laugh, discover, contemplate, or commune with friends and family happened, but it was the exception, not the rule. Now I appreciate that developing leisure skills is just as important, if not more so, as being able to excel at new tasks at work. We may talk about work-life balance but I only understood its full meaning when the work part of the equation was missing. It would have been exceptional to have realized this before I transitioned out of work!

A Relationship With Money

I attended a seminar a few years back and the speaker asked the audience, "What is your relationship with money?" That question stopped me in my tracks and I wondered, "What is she talking about? Do I have money? Do I want money? Do I need money? What constitutes a relationship with money?"

A relationship with money, as with people, is about knowing the value that that relationship brings. It is, by nature, not a quantitative relationship but a qualitative one. Good relationships are based on reciprocal good or value.

A relationship with money means knowing where you stand with it, how you value it, what you want from it. That's quite different from the dollar value of a financial plan, a pension, or a 401K.

It is a dynamic balance to ensure that the value of money never overshadows the value of self. In other words, if you defer your well-being to how much money you have, you may always feel "less" than what you have or want, than others around you, or where others perceive you should be. Instead, a healthy relationship with money allows you to make choices, take direction, and value yourself first, using the resources you have to support those choices.

Don't get me wrong. Money and financial planning is essential. It is one of the first retirement building blocks. You need to foster relationships and connections with a financial planner, credit union, bank, and tax accountant. These connections may help determine what you can and cannot do, where you live, what you eat, how often you travel, or what you wear. But it will not define who you are.

So what is the number, the amount you need for retirement? Ask your financial planner but a determined amount of money might never be enough. Some close friends waited and waited to have children because they felt they didn't have enough money and hadn't reached their financial goals. They ended up never having children at all because, quite simply, they felt that there never seemed to be enough as their financial goals had not been reached.

One of my clients spoke to me about a 75-year-old friend of hers who was so lonely and unable to find purpose after he left his business and his wife passed away. A well-educated, active, articulate, and healthy man, he was suddenly lost and sedentary, seeming to lack the luster that had defined his long and productive life. And, by the way, he was a billionaire.

Prepare for your financial future but you can be just as whole with $50 as you can with $500. You remain who you are, espousing your own purpose and values. You might need to eat tuna sandwiches instead of gourmet sushi, but how much value do you place on eating fish anyway? As a single retiree, this concept at times seems daunting. I mean, who wants to go out to dinner with friends for a tuna sandwich? But, alas, you might be surprised at how the value of money seems to decrease as the value of self increases. Put a little aioli on that tuna sandwich!

Embracing Vulnerability And Seeking Support

When I contemplated my own retirement journey, I realized that what I was describing was not dissimilar to the process of recovery from an addiction. A very close friend is a recovering alcoholic, and what he has gone through, and continues to embrace, is facing his own vulnerability — the need to take one day at a time and surround himself with support resources. We have had many conversations about the parallels between recovery from addiction and recovery from the absence of work.

My addiction and resulting lack of identity was not as a result of substance, but rather the loss of work. The recovery process has been my own retirement — finding a purpose greater than and without work.

The loss, uncertain future, and newly freed up substantial amounts of unscheduled time, tend to be problematic to both my recovering alcoholic friend and myself. We both realized that we needed to manage our time, make a plan to refocus our lives daily with purpose and verve.

I have also emulated how he seeks out support and networking, giving himself permission to have a sponsor (someone who has been where he treads and is willing to provide guidance and lessons). He speaks with others in recovery to gain insight, consider options, and to learn from the story of others.

I refer to these different levels of support, also needed during retirement, as retirement alliances or connections to formulate a personal "retirement team". As with any recovery, retirement requires a network that provides touch points for contemplation, decision-making, and viable and challenging options to and through retirement. In a nutshell, retirement necessitates seeking support.

Close and empathetic friends, family, church, professional or leisure networks, social media, classes, hobbies, other retirees, publications, health and financial service providers, real estate brokers, communities or community centers — and, yes, a retirement coach, therapist, or marriage counselor — all offer different types of support to guide you towards a constructive and meaningful retirement.

Couples know this to be true as spousal connections are not always easy in retirement. Often, clearly articulating a common view of life after work with partners is overlooked while planning for retirement. But I would suggest celebrating the good fortune of being able to hold such a spousal conversation to plan the future together.

Am I Really Enough?

I was speaking with a Pilates instructor who rather nonchalantly suggested that I find my *ikigai*. I responded that, yes I really should, although had no idea what I was committing myself to or that I had even lost it in the first place.

After a quick Google search, I discovered that one's *ikigai*, or what has been referred to as a joyous purpose, is a Japanese tradition to know why you wake up in the morning, the purpose of your life, and your own personal value and legacy.

It's your inner Zen, your hot yoga, your Tai Chi, your confession, your walk on the beach, your trek through the woods, or your sunset. It's the ability to find your own peace. And yes, I had lost it.

When I was in my 20s, I remember visiting friends for the holidays. Their 5-year-old enjoyed lots of holiday gifts and my friends were rather boastful of how happy they had made their child. But shortly thereafter, the child became rather distant, withdrawn, and teary.

I took the child for a short walk and discovered that the malaise was caused by him not having presents to give to his parents.

So, the child had not only judged the day based solely on receiving so many great gifts, but on his own wherewithal to reciprocate — to give back. This was astounding to me. So we ran off, found some knick-knacks and wrapped them.

The child, with a huge smile, a cessation of tears, and somehow a feeling of confidence and self-worth, offered the gifts to his parent, who, of course, accepted them with great delight.

I never forgot that morning and how giving back was so deeply experienced by a child. Little did I know then that some 40 years later, after a successful and fulfilling life of many gifts from many people over many years, I, too, would need to figure out how to give back.

The journey through retirement is iterative. Just when I think I have it figured out, something changes. As I age, the challenges that emerge are new and different than those I have previously experienced. Am I modeling the values I believe in? Can I re-invent myself? Do I move? Will I remain healthy? Should I spend more time with aging family members? Should I start dating? Do I work or volunteer? Should I sail to Portugal?

As a single retiree, the way I face new challenges that emerge during retirement is by valuing support from others, embracing my own vulnerability, and actively recognizing and enacting my own values, purpose, creativity, and renewal. Having the opportunity to make choices is, after all, the greatest of gifts.

So I was not surprised when Skyping with a friend, who is also a life coach, that he remarked, "I know who you are and what you believe. I know what you have done in your life and to whom and how you have contributed to others. So, do you see what you — a single, vulnerable, 60+ year old — have to offer to yourself and to others at this time of your life that you are calling "retirement"? You asked the question, and you are the answer. Your best resource for a continued healthy, resilient, and fulfilling life is you.

You get to celebrate your own values. You get to make plans, give back to, and receive from others. You get to discover new relationships and new places. You get to hang out at the gym. You get to celebrate your accomplishments. You get to blow out more birthday candles. You get to foster a robust, dynamic, and sustainable curiosity — every day. Are you getting this?"

About The Author

Douglas Passanisi holds a doctorate in adult education and is a retired United Nations international civil servant, serving nearly 20 years in southern Africa and New York. He has been an instructor and workshop facilitator at the UN Staff College, and at universities in the United States, France, and Mozambique. He is a team diagnostics trainer and coach, a professional certified retirement coach, a contributor to the Retirement Resource, a member of Retirement Options, a founding member of the Retirement Coaches Association, and founder of SeguestoRetirement.com. He is currently based in New York City.

How To Create True Wealth In Retirement

By Beau Henderson

According to a 2018 Retirement Confidence Survey conducted by the Employee Benefit Research Institute with Greenwald and Associates, only 17% of Americans say they are "very confident" that they will have enough money to live comfortably throughout retirement.[1]

It seems that a lot of people are feeling uneasy about their ability to retire with enough wealth during retirement. To address this, most financial advisors focus on the money. Experts crunch the numbers and tell people what to invest in and how much to save, advocating for nest eggs somewhere north of $1 million.

Meanwhile, the news about living longer and retiring earlier with fewer sources of guaranteed income keeps getting worse. The bursting of the dot-com bubble in 2001 and the Great Recession of 2008 gave investors on Wall Street a bumpy and prolonged ride straight through market hell and back again.

Those who stayed invested and survived are only just now recovering, and many people are wondering what will happen next and what to do. No wonder only 17% of workers feel confident in their ability to live comfortably during retirement.

While I'm certainly not against the idea of a healthy nest egg and I advocate for a robust savings plan,

I've learned that securing true wealth is not just about following the money. In fact, if that is all you do to prepare for retirement, you'll likely end up with very little wealth at all, even if you retire during a bull market with millions in the bank. I have a different way of looking at wealth, and what I learned changed the course of my career, the way I do retirement planning, the way I talk to my clients; it even changed the investment priorities in my own life.

The True Story Of The Miserable Millionaire

Back when I was in my 20s and 30s, I believed in this idea of following the money. I bought wholeheartedly into the idea that being rich is defined by money, power, and fancy-schmancy stuff like mansions, suits, and luxury cars. Then, one day, I met Richard.

Richard had it all — money (wheelbarrows full), power (because cash influences), and stuff (a jaw-dropping mansion featured in *Better Homes and Gardens*, with a stable of classic cars, an art collection, a rolling, green, and manicured lawn, etc.).

Whatever my young impressionable mind could imagine as the definition of true wealth, Richard owned. He had followed the money and created a life filled with every luxury that money could buy and, boy, I really couldn't wait to meet him.

I remember the night well. On my way to his house, driving in my new but not-yet-paid-for car, I was convinced that I, too, was on the same path he had taken. I, too, was following the money, and part of me was actually hoping that some kind of magical, golden fairy dust would rub off on me before the night was over.

I drove through the entrance gate to Richard's estate, wound up the long driveway past the opulent grounds and parked my car. I walked up to the front door in my polished shoes to introduce myself, pausing for just a moment to take it all in, bask in the glory, breathe in the tantalizing aromas of all this wealth. Oh yeah, baby! Definitely my kind of smells.

I knocked on the giant wooden door. It was opened by a gaunt, haggard-looking old man. Probably his father, I thought, or maybe the butler. You can only imagine my absolute and utter astonishment when he introduced himself to me as Richard.

"So nice to meet you, Beau," he said. "Come on in, won't you?"

Richard was not an old man in years. By my calculations, he had to be in his early 60s, but he shuffled when he walked, barely able to stand up straight. He was stiff and frail looking as he led me through his spacious but cold house filled with gorgeous but inanimate things.

We sat in his study, his hands bone thin as they gripped the arms of his chair. A nurse brought him a glass of water and his pills. I learned that he'd just come home from the hospital and was recovering after having suffered a massive heart attack. The nurse left us to talk and, to this day, I remember the silence of her footsteps as she left us alone, followed by the deafening quiet of the house. It was like being in a tomb — like no one really lived there at all. If that house had ever known laughter, it was long gone by then. The walls loomed, rich and silent, as Richard told me about his business and his life. Not once did he smile.

His story? Richard was divorced three times with four kids, none of whom would visit or even speak to him on the phone, and had few friends. It was a true miracle that he had survived the heart attack, but his health was in shambles. There was a long list of things he wasn't supposed to eat, drink, or do. His first ex-wife told him, "Serves you right." Really, she wasn't at all surprised.

Richard looked out at the quiet mahogany walls of his study and when he finished his story, he made a gesture with his hands. "This is what it all comes down to," he said. And I looked down at his empty hands and saw that everything of any real value to him had been lost.

I drove home that night deep in thought. It was a shock to see how unhappy Richard was, even with all of his monetary success. It was kind of like being told that there was no Santa Claus.

A few days later, I had an appointment with another client — a regular, middle-class guy and his wife. Mark had called me up, looking for advice about how to create a modest, fixed-income during retirement for him and his wife. When I arrived at their house, the smells were warm and rich and I was glad when they invited me to stay for dinner. Throughout the meal and afterward, his adult children and grandchildren were stopping by, dropping things off or just saying, "Hi."

There was a lot of laughter, teasing, and storytelling as they introduced themselves and each other. They were all so happy and familiar with one another, they were finishing each other's sentences. Their house was comfortable, filled with laughter and the sounds of little feet. When I left for the evening, Mark walked me to the door.

"So," he said, "do you think you can help me and my wife do this thing called retirement?"

"Absolutely," I assured him, but all the while I was thinking, "Buddy, you've already got the important parts figured out. My help will be the easy part."

Investments For A Rich Life

What I realized after meeting with Richard was that I was following the wrong path. I had thought that I knew about investing for true wealth, but I was only considering half of the equation. My model considered only physical assets and not the human ones. So I put together a new model — one that is much needed in today's retirement planning industry.

This new model for retirement planning focuses not just on income planning and asset allocation, but on the non-financial aspects of retirement that give us greater life satisfaction. Study after study confirms that achieving happiness during retirement isn't just about the money.

It's about having a balance of those other assets that sometimes even money can't buy. These assets include our health and the creation of meaningful experiences. They also include investments in relationships that are important to us.

It's not that money is bad or that it can ruin a person's life. It's that you have to know what to do with it and how to integrate it with all the other aspects of true wealth.

How do you integrate the hard and fast rules of good financial planning with the softer side of human needs? What kinds of questions should you be asking yourself, and what kinds of things should you be doing? Helping people to achieve a healthy balance of both financial and non-physical assets became my mission and true calling when I founded my firm, RichLife Advisors. It's why I became a retirement planning specialist.

A Focus On Experiences, Not Things

After giving a talk in San Diego, my Uber driver was taking me back to my hotel and he started talking about his retirement. He had just left his job at the gas plant with a great pension and he was in good financial shape. But a few months into retirement, he found himself taking two and three naps a day. He realized that he was tired because he was bored and that without his job and the social interactions he had among his friends at work, he was no longer having the kinds of meaningful life experiences that he desired.

So, he got a side gig as an Uber driver. Now he gets to travel to different places and meet new people almost every day. He may not be living the traditional version of retirement, but he's enjoying his life and has been happy ever since.

My friend, the Uber driver, is not alone in finding value in working during retirement. According to a landmark study by Merrill Lynch about the new retirement workscape, we've reached the tipping point where the majority of people in retirement will continue to work, often in new and surprising ways.[2]

But they aren't necessarily working because they need the money. The 2012 United States of Aging survey conducted telephone interviews among Americans aged 50 and older and found that 76% of seniors say they are staying in the workforce because of productivity, and 70% do it for enjoyment.[3]

We might have a stereotype in our minds of the ideal retirement being filled with passive activities in reclining poses, amid a backdrop of palm trees and beaches or cruise ships. You may also have a definition of true wealth that conjures up pictures of Scrooge backstroking through his piles of gold coins. My clients over the years have shown me that retirement doesn't have to look like a magazine ad to be enjoyable. Because of them, I've come to a different understanding of what true wealth really is. True wealth includes meaningful experiences with loved ones and friends.

Retirement can give you the opportunity to re-evaluate what kinds of experiences you want to intentionally create for yourself. Any experience we plan for ourselves, regardless of how much it costs, has the potential to become a lifelong memory. It's these memories that we turn over and over in our minds more than we turn over actual gold coins.

Memories cannot be taxed, stolen, or lost in a lawsuit, nor do they depreciate over time. In fact, the more they are withdrawn, and told over and over again, the better they get. There is no penalty, withdrawals can be made as early as the next day, and doing so only makes them stronger. What other asset can boast this kind of return?

It's our memories that become our most valued treasure, a finding confirmed by a research article published by the *Journal of Consumer Psychology* that did research on the benefits of spending money on doing things rather than on having things.

The studies find that spending our money on experiences such as a walk in the woods or a trip to the beach brings us greater happiness than spending money on material purchases. This rings especially true for me because my best memories include the 10 years during which my dad spent coaching my football team. My dad ran his own business and, when I was growing up, he often worked seven days a week, but he still made it a priority to spend time with me. His presence out there on the field every day after school told me that I was worth it and that I was important. That said more and meant more to me than any physical thing that he could have bought for me.

A unique experience can be as simple as a trip to the batting cages or breakfast in the backyard. Look for these opportunities during retirement to create memories with the people important in your life.

Find out what makes them light up, what they find interesting, or share with them what you find to be of value. Being intentional about the experiences you create for yourself can give you a double deposit into your wealth accounts — money in the bank and memories in the mind.

Investing In People During Retirement

My dad passed away when I was 23, making all those hours he invested in me even more valuable. Although the average lifespan has gotten longer and we are spending more years during retirement than ever before, no one has the promise of tomorrow. That's why I also advocate for intentional investments in the people who are most important in our lives. During retirement, we have more time than ever before to invest in others. The funny thing is, we might not know exactly where to begin.

Recently, I met with a Texas couple who retired this year and needed some help setting up an income plan. I asked the husband, Jim, "So how's retirement going?" He said, "Great, Beau! It's going great. I'm really enjoying it."

A few minutes later when we were walking into the restaurant, his wife pulled me aside and quickly whispered, "Beau, you have to help Jim find another job or a hobby because he's driving me crazy!"

This is not at all uncommon. After spending a lifetime employed as an engineer, teacher, or graphic designer, people retire and then they have to ask themselves, "Who are we in retirement?" For married couples, this is times two, with the added question of, "How well do we really know each other?"

I talk a lot with couples about the money conversations they should have at different stages of their life. Before you retire, there are financial questions that have to be answered.

But before you can use your money to fund your goals, you have to first identify what's important to you and to each other. You need to set aside some time to find out if your spouse wants to start a business, take up painting, or begin a second career, for example.

For most people, the majority of social situations revolve around work relationships. Once that aspect of your life is gone, you have to identify how things will shift. Are you building relationships with people outside of work so that the transition into retirement doesn't leave you feeling isolated? Are you investing time in your spouse so that you still feel close to each other once the time of retirement comes? Or are you relying on them too much to fill a void in your life?

Think about how the dynamics with the people you are closest to in your life will change or shift during retirement. Sit down with your spouse or, better yet, make an evening of it by planning for a date or a meaningful experience. Sit out on the deck with a bottle of wine or make a reservation at your favorite neighborhood restaurant — whatever would mean something to you, take the time to create an experience for yourself.

Then, have the conversation that people forget to have. Talk with your spouse about the kinds of things do you want to be doing in retirement and what will make you happy. Then, craft your income plan around that.

As my client, Richard, taught me, without those non-financial pieces in place, all the money in the world won't be able to fill up the holes that the loss of those things creates. The good news is that you can plan for success in retirement by being intentional about the kinds of experiences you want to create for yourself, and the people with whom you will be doing these things.

Don't just focus on the finances. Make time to invest in your human assets — your own health included — and you'll be one step closer to achieving the definition of what I call true wealth.

About the Author

Beau Henderson, RICP®, WMCP®, NSSA®, CLTC®, CRPC is a retirement consultant, money and business coach, best-selling author, podcast host, and CEO of RichLife Advisors. As an advocate for retirement literacy and a pioneer of the integrated approach to "The New Retirement," he continues to provide resources and tools for navigating both the financial and non-financial aspects of a successful retirement through his best-selling books, podcast, and national consulting, speaking, and television appearances. Visit www.RichLifeAdvisors.com.

Notes

1. *2018 Retirement Confidence Survey*, April 24, 2018, https://www.ebri.org/pdf/surveys/rcs/2018/2018RCS_Report_V5MGAchecked.pdf

2. Merrill Lynch, *Work In Retirement: Myths and Motivations*, 2014, https://agewave.com/wp-content/uploads/2016/07/2014-ML-AW-Work-in-Retirement_Myths-and-Motivations.pdf

3. National Council on Aging, *The United States of Aging Survey*, 2012, https://www.aarp.org/content/dam/aarp/livable-communities/learn/research/the-united-states-of-aging-survey-2012-aarp.pdf

4. Amit Kumar and Thomas Gilovich, "To Do or to Have, Now or Later? The Preferred Consumption Profiles of Material and Experiential Purchases," *Journal of Consumer Psychology* 26, no. 2 (2016): https://static1.squarespace.com/static/5394 dfa6e4b0d7fc44700a04/t/55bd5d88e4b0dc 628beb187e/1438473608584/Kumar+Gilov ich+%28in+press%29+To+Do+or+To+Hav e+Now+or+Later+JCP.pdf

Facing Forced Retirement: Getting Upright When Your World Turns Upside Down

By Phyllis Diamond, LCSW

What Is Forced Retirement?

If you are reading this chapter either you or someone close to you had or is about to have a personal experience with forced or involuntary retirement. What makes a forced retirement different from normal retirement is who decides to terminate the employment relationship. The ending of your employment was not directly of your choosing and you are retiring earlier than you expected. You are not alone! About 47% of current retirees were forced into unplanned retirement because of layoffs, taking care of sick parents or spouses, or their own illnesses.

In an era of company downsizing and consolidation, it is not uncommon for older and more highly paid employees who have been with the company for many years to be put on the chopping block. If you are fortunate enough to be with a large company, you might be given a retirement package. These "golden handcuffs" are usually one-time offers that are difficult to refuse. Despite the financial incentive, the prospective retiree likely would have elected to retire later. Therefore, a post-employment plan would not be in place.

Being laid off is even more difficult for the individual who is not given a retirement package and is now also struggling with being unprepared for the additional financial burden of an earlier than planned retirement. Even if there has been good financial planning, the additional unexpected years of unemployment puts a significant strain on life-style choices.

Health insurance coverage is a particularly difficult challenge for those forced to retire before age 65 when they are eligible for Medicare. Paying for medical insurance for you and your spouse through COBRA or the open market can be an unexpected financial hardship.

If you had to retire because of health issues or to care for an infirmed family member, it may seem to the outside world that you chose to retire. Research has shown that this is not the reality. The decision to retire is still coming from outside circumstances, and not of one's choosing. It is often a painful decision, especially when you are still at the height of your career, but one you feel forced to make.

Gary is a 63-year-old married photojournalist who was forced to retire two years ago. He loved his work, which was with several prominent magazines. He had an exciting career covering major world events. As the print news business began to contract, Gary lost his full-time position and began freelance work in other parts of the media industry. His insufficient skills in the growing online environment put him at a disadvantage.

Over time, he was getting fewer assignments and was required to work terrible hours for less pay.

Gary found the work demoralizing. He attributed this to his age and to the changing nature of the news business. He felt rejected. Gary had not wanted to retire — rather, he felt the industry retired him.

His wife owned a successful business and was not ready to give it up. They had a lot of conflicts about her expectations of the "honey-do list" now that he was no longer working. Gary felt like he'd lost his identity as a competent photojournalist and was being relegated to menial household tasks. His days felt empty. He wanted to travel and spend time in a warmer climate, but his wife's business made that difficult.

Most of all, he didn't like having to depend on her financially. He couldn't figure out how to structure his time or find something meaningful in his life.

Diane is 65 and was committed to her job as a research analyst for an investment bank. She felt she could work until her 70s. She had been there a long time, was excellent at her job, and always had good reviews.

In 2015 the bank was undergoing financial problems and did massive layoffs. Diane was shocked when she got a pink slip. She was not ready to retire. A divorced woman, she had saved for retirement, so she was not worried about finances.

But all her friends were still working, and she feared the isolation of retirement. By her own admission, Diane was not much of a risk taker and uncomfortable meeting new people. While she loved to travel, none of her friends could join her and she couldn't imagine going on a group tour with people she did not know.

She did some volunteer work but was concerned that her life wouldn't have much meaning without her job. Diane felt like she'd lost her purpose in life.

These two forced retirees feel like they've lost their equilibrium. Individuals who face involuntary retirement were found to have the lowest life satisfaction scores as compared to those who made a voluntary departure from the work force, according to a 2013 study on the Impact of Types of Retirement Transitions on Perceived Satisfaction with Life.[1]

When Your World Turns Upside Down

The loss of a career can feel like a death. The resulting grieving process is similar to that following the death of a friend or loved one. Elizabeth Kübler-Ross has written extensively about death and dying. She outlines five stages in the process of grieving a loss.[2]

Denial — Anger — Bargaining — Depression — Acceptance

The first stage is denial or shock. You can't believe this is really happening. You feel paralyzed.

The second stage is anger. Once the shock has worn off you begin to feel angry toward your company, supervisor, and the world. For many retirees, the job is how they define themselves. When this is taken away, they feel frustrated and angry that they've lost their identity.

The third stage is bargaining. This is where you might want to try to get your job back, even with reduced pay, hours, or responsibilities. It rarely works.

The fourth stage is depression. The reality can no longer be denied. Feelings of hopelessness and helplessness take hold and the future looks very bleak.

The last stage is acceptance. When your anger and depression are no longer consuming, you accept your new reality and begin to develop plans to make the most of your life. Each individual passes through these stages at his or her own rate and may move back and forth through some of the stages.

A major problem of forced retirement is the lack of time to plan because of the suddenness of the termination. While there is certainly an impact on financial planning, our focus here is on non-financial life planning.

When one voluntarily retires there has been time to think about the future. Do they want to kick back and have a leisure filled retirement? Do they plan to continue in some form of work or volunteerism? Is there some life passion they've been waiting to fulfill? The forced retiree hasn't had the chance to think in advance about the opportunities retirement

76

can afford them. Retirement looks like a blank canvas they haven't yet learned how to paint!

Work provides us with five important functions the forced retiree will suddenly lose. How will you deal with the changes in your financial situation? What about the time management and structure to your day that has been a major part of your working life? What will happen to the status you had and the recognition, reputation and sense of achievement that came with it? Where will you find the sense of usefulness you felt at your job? And how do you replace the social connections that are gone from your everyday life?

These losses can lead to feelings of emptiness and a sense that there is nothing engaging with which to look forward.

Emotional Whiplash

The emotional risks of forced retirement are well documented. Forced retirees often feel shame about their sudden exit from the work force. You may be embarrassed to tell people you are no longer working. You worry about what others might be thinking about you. It can make you feel like a failure.

Individuals retiring involuntarily are more likely than others to suffer depressive symptoms. The psychic benefits that might arise from the reduced stress or pressure of not working are outweighed by factors such as loss of social connectedness or the other work-related positives.

Depressive symptoms can include a feeling of hopelessness, worthlessness, helplessness, guilt, fatigue, changes in sleep patterns and appetite, loss of interest in things once pleasurable (including sex), irritability, restlessness, and trouble concentrating.

These feelings will often pass once you regain your equilibrium. If you feel stuck in a depressed mood it will help to talk with a mental health professional.

In addition to feelings of depression, forced retirees often suffer from increased anxiety. An excellent description of anxiety is the overestimation of danger and the underestimation of your ability to cope. It is natural to feel frightened about what lies ahead. Forced retirement can feel like you are at the edge of a cliff and the wind can throw you over at any minute. You may not feel like you have the inner strength to withstand the forces that could topple you.

Anxious symptoms can be characterized by feelings of tension, worry, and recurring intrusive thoughts and concerns. People with high levels of anxiety can have physical reactions like increased blood pressure, tightness in their chests, nausea, and headaches. Anxiety generally subsides when the new retiree takes action steps to create a satisfying retirement.

When a forced retiree has not been able to move past depression and/or anxiety, the overwhelming feelings may be more than he or she wants to bear. The danger is that some people will turn to alcohol, drugs, gambling or other addictions to avoid feeling the emptiness of their lives.

There has been an increased prevalence of substance abuse in the elderly, often the result of feeling that they are no longer valued by society and that they have nothing more to contribute. The use of substances feels like a quick fix to life's disappointments, but the impact on family relationships, health, and quality of life is a big price to pay.

The forced retiree is not the only one to suffer from sudden unemployment. It has a major impact on relationships between couples. Retirement in general can pose challenges to couples that need to make adaptations to new roles and responsibilities. When the couple is thrown into sudden retirement, there has been no time to discuss these changes in advance. It becomes a trial by fire.

Conflict is often the means through which changes are made rather than through planned conversation. Tensions can run high and the forced retiree feels more guilt for having brought this on his family. If the husband has been forced out of his job, he may feel like he's not pulling his financial weight. He may feel that his sense of himself as a man has been diminished.

If his wife continues to work, there can be resentment about the new household tasks he's expected to take on. He may feel inadequate to meet demands that held no interest to him in the past. The stress of these conflicts can compound the feeling of loss experienced by both partners.

Getting Upright

The first step to managing the life-altering event of forced retirement is to recognize that you are not alone. The feelings described above are normal for anyone who has had to leave the work force involuntarily.

You have been forced to leave work because business or life circumstances have made it unfeasible for you to stay. You are allowed to grieve. It is important to give yourself time to sit with the feelings, even though it's uncomfortable. Feelings that don't get processed tend to come out when you least expect it.

You don't want to kick the dog because you're angry at your situation. Keeping your feelings to yourself may make them feel larger than life. Talk to your spouse, friends, or other family members. You can ask them to listen, but let them know that you would prefer that they don't give you advice. Everyone will have an opinion about your situation, but it is usually based on their own life experience, not yours. Only you will be able to figure out what comes next. Don't rush into something out of fear. Impulsive actions don't always turn out the way you expect. Now is the time to just think and feel.

Breathe! Sounds simple, right! Relaxed breathing is one of the best tools to deal with stress. It slows down your heart rate and anxious thoughts. I like a simple breathing exercise of inhaling through your nose to the count of four and exhale through your mouth to the count of four.

Concentrate on the counting or the feeling of the breath coming in and out of your lungs. That focus keeps your mind occupied instead of thinking about your worries. It helps to practice relaxation breathing for a couple of minutes twice a day. Then use it whenever the stress of your situation feels overwhelming.

Another helpful technique for dealing with anxiety is called "worry time." Schedule a 15- to 30-minute time each day to do your worrying. (Avoid bedtime when it can interfere with sleep.) When a worry comes up at other times of the day, tell yourself to save it for your worry time. It will be hard at first, but don't give up. During worry time allow yourself to do as much worrying as you need, and then let it go until the next day. In this way you can clear your head and function better during the rest of the day.

This is also a good time to start a journal. Even if you are not much of a writer, it doesn't matter. Write down any of the thoughts and feeling that come to you. Don't censor what you write. Allow it to be a "mind dump." While you are writing, if an idea, dream, or passion comes to you, let it flow. Writing it down doesn't need to compel you into action. These thoughts and feelings can become a reference point for you at some time in the future.

Once the feelings and emotions associated with your new situation have sunk in, action is a good antidote to anxiety and depression. You may feel like you don't want to get moving. You might want to linger longer in feeling upset.

However, if a lot of time has gone by, and your family and friends are beginning to bug you for not taking action, it's probably time to get moving. Most people think that action requires motivation. In truth, it works the other way around.

Once you begin to take action, even when you don't want to, you will feel more like continuing to move. Take micro steps. It is too overwhelming to imagine changing your whole life. Your journal can be a first action step. If isolation is one of your fears, first make a list of people you might meet for lunch; then make a date with someone (anyone).

If you don't know where to begin to find volunteer opportunities, pick one interest from your journal and begin by Googling volunteer possibilities in your community. Each small step brings you closer to achieving your goals.

One of the scariest feelings about suddenly being retired is creating structure to your days. Without work, it's all on your shoulders to figure out how you would like your days to look.

You might want to write down the hours of the day with a blank space next to each hour. Then, begin filling in what an ideal day would look like. It is a useful reference point even if your actual days don't follow it precisely.

Planning the beginning of your day is most important. That is often the most difficult time of day when it feels like you have the whole empty day in front of you. While reading the newspaper cover to cover might have appeal in the beginning of your retirement, it may soon become boring and getting up and out might be a better option.

Do an activity that makes you feel like you've accomplished something. Whether it's some form of exercise or meeting a friend, it's extremely important that you get out of the house. Once you engage in a morning activity it is likely to lead to more activities to do throughout your day.

Finding a community to replace the lost social engagements provided by your job is of utmost value when you've been forced to retire. We all need to feel connected to something. It isn't easy to enter a new group and start up conversations with strangers unless you are an extrovert.

Try to remember that most people feel the same way and welcome others approaching them. Look for anyone standing alone. You are both in the same boat. People find new communities through religious organizations, classes, volunteering, exercise programs, etc. The choice is yours. Take the action step!

Rita is a 66-year-old woman who worked in market research. She was forced to retire at 55 when the small firm she worked for was sold to a larger competitor. Soon after, her husband had to relocate for his job. She liked her career, but the idea of starting over in a new city was daunting.

Her husband had a successful career and she did not have to work. She began exploring part-time jobs when the financial crises hit. The job market dried up and Rita decided that it wasn't fair to take a job away from someone who really needed it. She was now in a new city where she knew no one and had nothing to fill up her days.

Adrift after two years, she became depressed and couldn't see her way out of it. Finally a friend suggested she see a retirement coach. Rita began exploring what would enrich her retirement life.

She discovered that she needed to get out of the house every morning. She joined a Jewish Community Center where she began taking exercise classes four mornings a week. She took bridge lessons, joined a choral group, and began socializing with the women she met there.

A volunteer position with a local congresswoman has enabled her to use some of her marketing skills. Eleven years into retirement, Rita is feeling very content with her life.

If you've been forced to retire because of illness or disability, or the need to care for a sick relative, it might feel like your life has limited options. You may not be able to engage in the activities that you enjoyed in the past.

You may have to give up some of your dreams because of time commitments demanded by caretaking responsibilities or diminished capacity to engage in certain activities because of physical limitations. These are losses that you will grieve.

However, it is important not to get stuck there. To have a satisfying retirement it is necessary to refocus on what you still have in your life rather than what you've lost.

If you've had to retire because of disability recognize that you are more than your body. Growing in other directions through such pursuits as education, engagement in some form of voluntarism, or finding a passion to pursue can expand life in retirement.

In his book, *The New Retirement*, Dr. Richard Johnson talks about the importance of vitality. It means, "Living to the fullest extent possible, under whatever conditions are presented to you."[3] Focus on what enhances you rather than what tears you down.

If retirement is due to caretaking responsibilities, what is most important is taking care of you! Efforts should be made to find time to engage in pleasurable activities that meet your needs independent of that of your relative — and don't feel guilty about it! You will have more energy and emotional resources to care for others when you pay attention to yourself.

How do you make lemonade out of lemons? Involuntarily having to leave your job is a life lemon, but finding new opportunities in retired life can be your lemonade.

You can rediscover or find new passions that you never had time to pursue. You will have the time to devote to improving your health and wellness. You might even decide to explore new work possibilities now that you are in control of how much you want to work. It can also be a time to take classes in areas of interest.

Forced retirement presents more complicated challenges than those faced by individuals who choose their retirement date. You begin with a rocky road of shock, unexpected loss, grief and destabilization.

However, once you find your footing you will discover that retirement doesn't have to be an ending. It can be a time for personal growth and self-actualization, a new engagement with life and rediscovered dreams.

About The Author

Phyllis Diamond is founder of Strategic Retirement Coaching. She has 40 years of experience helping clients break through the barriers that keep them from achieving their life goals. Trained as a Licensed Clinical Social Worker, she is in private practice as a psychotherapist in New York City specializing in helping individuals and couples manage major life transitions. A Certified Retirement Coach since 2010, Phyllis has coached corporate executives, entrepreneurs, lawyers, media professionals, educators and others to find fulfillment in their retirement years. She is an experienced retirement workshop leader and is on the board of the Retirement Coaches Association. Her website is Strategicretirementcoaching.com.

Notes

1. Douglas A. Hershey and Kène Henkens, "Impact of Different Types of Retirement Transitions on Perceived Satisfaction with Life," *The Gerontologist* 54, no. 2 (2013), doi:10.1093/geront/gnt006.

2. Elisabeth Kübler-Ross, *On Death and Dying* (New York: MacMillan, 1969).

3. Richard P. Johnson, *The New Retirement: Discovering Your Dream* (St. Louis, MO: Retirement Options, 2001

Developing Resilience for a Thriving Retirement

By Reid Stone

What is Resilience?

Throughout our lives we have encountered good times and bad — the ebbs and flows of life. Some people encounter more or tougher challenges than others and each of us responds to these challenges differently. Some people are able to respond more positively than others. You have likely received your share of bumps and bruises along life's journey up to this point in your life. The longer we live, the more bumps and bruises we will receive.

In response to life's challenges, you've picked yourself up, dusted yourself off, and continued moving forward. You didn't have much choice — life moves on whether we are ready or not. Sheryl Sandburg, COO of Facebook and founder of Leanin.org, has this take on resilience: "I think we build resilience to prepare for whatever adversity we'll face. And we all face some adversity — we're all living some form of Option B."[1]

Merriam-Webster defines resilience as "the ability to recover from or adjust easily to misfortune or change." *Psychology Today* defines resilience "as that ineffable quality that allows some people to be knocked down by life and come back stronger than ever. Rather than letting failure overcome them and drain their resolve, they find a way to rise from the ashes." More succinctly, it is typically thought of as a person's ability to bounce back after dealing with a setback.

Why Resilience Is Important During Retirement

Much of the research on resilience is focused on how to develop this skill in children to prepare them for the inevitable challenges they face in childhood, and to prepare for them for adulthood. One of the primary advantages of developing resilience at a younger age is having additional time and energy to recover from a setback.

Having more time gives us a chance to gather ourselves, change course, and take the opportunity to make a fundamental change in our lives — making a leap forward rather than simply bouncing back.

Even during middle age, we have time and energy that allows us to make a positive change. In retirement, we may not have the same amount of time ahead of us or energy that we did earlier in our lives.

However, we oftentimes overlook that we still may have one quarter to one third of our lives left to live in retirement. We still have a lot of life to live and a great deal to offer from our experience and knowledge gained.

As behavioral scientist, author and speaker, Dr. Steve Maraboli stated, "Life doesn't get easier or more forgiving; we get stronger and more resilient."[2]

Moving forward after a setback is more important in retirement when the setback can be even more severe — mentally, physically, emotionally, and/or spiritually than when we were younger.

When thinking about what retirement looks like, the path to a life with more freedom often appears idyllic. Most of what we read, see, and are told, is once we have planned financially, retirement will just fall into place and everything will be perfect.

Retirement can certainly be a time of great joy if both the financial *and* non-financial aspects are planned for and we are resilient in our quest to fulfill the vision we have for our retirement.

Unfortunately, for many retirees, the destination ends up looking and feeling much different than the idyllic life people envision for this time. In retirement, many changes occur — sometimes simultaneously — that create uncertainty, fear, anxiety, stress, and in extreme situations depression and substance abuse.

Moving toward and into this phase of our lives includes several different aspects, both financial and non-financial, that can throw us off-course as we strive to reach the retirement we want. Therefore, developing resilience is important to enjoy these later years.

From the experiences we have had to bounce back from throughout our lives — as both children and adults — we may feel prepared for any challenge or setback faced in retirement. After all, we have been through difficult challenges before and handled them just fine. Isn't retirement going to be perfect now that I can do what I want?

Perhaps, but retirement presents many challenges that are unique to this time in our lives. These challenges are often more difficult to prepare for, primarily because we either believe everything will be wonderful in retirement or because we were unaware of or didn't understand the variety of mental, physical, and social challenges that confront us during this time.

Some of the common challenges and setbacks people face prior to and during retirement that may not have come up earlier in life include job loss (either let go or forced retirement), death of a spouse or close friend(s), friends or family move away (loss of connections), moving ourselves (change of location), divorce, personal illness or health setback, change in social status or social circle, and rising stress (from uncertainty, lack of purpose, or negative thoughts).

To understand the importance of resilience in retirement and begin to develop resilience during this time, it is important to be aware of your current perception of retirement and to understand that retirement is a major life transition.

For many people, retirement has a negative connotation of being the beginning of the end. Viewing our life as phases, and seeing our retirement phase lasting 20 or more years, we need to adjust our thinking.

Retirement is the beginning of a new phase, one offering infinite options and possibilities. In the future, resilience will be even more important as medical and technological advances will push life expectancies past age 100.[3]

Further, we need to understand that retirement is a transition which takes time. A change is different than a transition. The change to retirement status can happen overnight. It begins the day after you stop doing what you have been doing for many years.

However, the process of planning and preparing for this status change called retirement is a transition that develops over time.

According to William Bridges, author of *Transitions*, these transitions begin with an ending, move to a neutral zone, and conclude with a new beginning. The ending involves letting go of old identity and ways while dealing with loss of identity, structure, and connections. The neutral zone is the time between moving from the old ways to the new beginning. It is a time of changing your thinking about the next phase. Beginnings are filled with a sense of optimism, energy, and possibilities. This time also involves developing a new identity and purpose for this time in your life.[4]

Resilience is important prior to and during the transition into retirement, as well as into the early years of retirement. The process of transitioning into retirement, being prepared to confront any challenges that might arise, and moving forward with confidence, can be defined as "Transitional Resilience."

Resilience and the Non-Financial Aspects of Retirement

Although there are many financial aspects of retirement that can occur and that have a need for us to be resilient, many of the more difficult challenges that require resilience are non-financial.

There are several ways to categorize the non-financial aspects of retirement. For our discussion of resiliency, I placed these non-financial aspects into the following categories:

Mental Resilience

This resilience is needed when we encounter setbacks in our work and coming up with a new purpose and identity. It is also needed when the dark side — the mental health challenges of depression, suicide and drug and alcohol abuse that can confront retirees.

Physical Resilience

This is the resilience needed when we have physical or health-related setbacks that keep us from reaching our health and fitness goals.

Social Resilience

This is the resilience that we need when faced with loneliness, isolation, and lack of strong connections or relationships.

Spiritual Resilience

This is the resilience that we need when our perception of retirement is negative, and we lose sight of meaning, values, and beliefs as we age. This commonly occurs later in life.

There are also several questions and concerns that come about prior to and into retirement that can cause negative thoughts and feelings. These questions and concerns fall into one of the resilience categories.

Here are a few of the primary questions and concerns pre-retirees and retirees have that cause uncertainty and fear about enjoying this phase of their life.

- What will I do now?

- What will make me happy during retirement?

- What will my purpose and identity be?

- How do I adjust to a new pace of daily life?

- How long will I live?

- How do my spouse and I get on the same page about various aspects of retirement?

This list of questions provides a starting point for beginning to understand some of the thoughts and concerns you are likely to encounter prior to and early on in your retirement transition.

These questions lead to other similar questions to help you create your ideal retirement. Understanding, giving thought to, and responding to these questions is one way to practice resilience.

If these and other questions are addressed in advance of retirement, we will be more aware of the possible challenges. It then becomes easier to handle the situation with a positive and confident approach which allows us to be resilient when these situations arise.

Ways to Practice and Develop Resilience

Although some people are naturally more resilient than others, resilience is something that can be practiced and learned. One way to practice and learn resilience is to be aware of situations that create stress for you or may result in a setback and apply responses to gain more control and confidence in these situations.

Gaining control allows you to slow down your thought process in response to the situation. This allows you to make an informed decision. Confidence allows you to move forward, knowing you are taking an approach to the situation that is both appropriate for you and likely to result in your success and happiness.

Here are 10 ways to practice and build resilience when life sets us back a few steps, especially as we work our way through retirement.

These strategies will help keep the setback from affecting us while also allowing us to bounce back (leap forward) quicker and with a clearer picture of what we want during this time in our life.

Change Your Perception Of Retirement

How we view retirement has a huge impact on how much we will enjoy this time. We can view it optimistically and enthusiastically, from the perspective that a breadth of opportunities lies ahead of us. Or we can choose to view retirement pessimistically, looking at this time as an ending with uncertainty and limited enthusiasm.

As we discussed earlier, retirement often carries with it a negative connotation as an ending. We need to change this thinking. It is also a time of transition. Transitions take time, while changes happen overnight. Take time to work through the transition into retirement and change your perception.

Do you view retirement with enthusiasm or with uncertainty and fear?

Create A Plan And Vision

Have a plan for what you will do with your time in retirement. The plan should include all aspects of your life including the mental, physical, social and spiritual.

Being able to visualize what this time will look like provides control of your life and confidence that you will attain the goals set in your plan.

In addition, it is important to set realistic goals and continue doing something each day to reach them. Making even small steps each day toward our goals keeps us engaged and gives us something to look forward to achieving.

Do you have a plan, and can you visualize your retirement?

Have A Purpose And Interests

Your plan and vision will include your purpose and interests. Because this is such a huge part of your vision for retirement, it stands on its own.

Having something you are passionate about that provides excitement gives you something to look forward to and keeps out negative thoughts. When we encounter a challenge or setback, our purpose and interests provide the driving force to keep us going.

What is your new purpose and what interests will you pursue during retirement?

Choose How You Respond To Situations

You choose how you respond to what happens in your life. When something unexpected happens, resilient people look at the situation with a positive outlook.

Additionally, when we run into challenges, we sometimes stop trying, usually because we aren't sure what to do next. We become paralyzed by the situation. Instead, look at the challenge as something to be overcome and conquered. Approaching it from this perspective makes it about creating a positive outcome.

When the situation has been conquered you will feel good about your accomplishment and derive strength from the experience.

How do you respond to challenges and setback in your life? Do you view them positively or negatively?

Maintain A Healthy And Active Lifestyle

Keeping and staying healthy and active is important to fully enjoy retirement. Being able to travel, play with grandkids, garden, golf, or other activities you enjoy requires us to be able to move.

Related to a healthy and active lifestyle are the lifestyle choices that put us at risk for health issues. For some, retirement can lead to alcohol abuse or drug addiction due to depression or the extra time we have. These habits often result from not having anything else productive to do in our life.

What things can you do to stay more healthy and active? Are you making wise lifestyle choices?

Develop Strong Relationships

Having strong relationships with friends and family is important for leading a happy and successful retirement. Having supportive relationships that offer encouragement and reassurance will help build your resilience.

Retirement can be a time of great change for our relationship with our spouse. We may not understand their thoughts and/or feelings, or what their dreams and goals are for this time. Spouses often end up spending much more time together than they used to in retirement, which can cause strife in the relationship.

Therefore, it is important that spouses discuss their hopes and dreams to make sure they are on the same page.

Who are your closest relationships? Can they offer support during your retirement transition? Have you and your spouse discussed what your shared retirement will look like?

Learn To Embrace Change

Retirement is likely to be quite different than when you had a more defined schedule and responsibilities. When our routine changes, we sometimes are "thrown off." Treat the change as an adventure — an opportunity to explore and learn new things.

Change provides an opportunity for us to grow and learn. This combined with our previous life experiences can be a powerful catalyst to something new and exciting. View change not as a setback, but rather as an opportunity to try something new.

Retirement is a time to try new experiences, activities, or things we have done previously that we want to do again.

We may find the first or second opportunity isn't what we expected or wanted. Use these times of change to hone in on what you really want to do and how you want to spend your time.

Are you willing to embrace change and accept the challenge to learn new things? What do you really want to do in retirement and how do you want to spend this time?

Look Inside Yourself To Find Direction

We often know what the right answer or approach is to a situation, either from instinct or prior experience. Trust your instincts about the right direction for you and keep moving forward.

When faced with a challenge, do you trust what you feel inside — what is your inner compass is telling you?

Get Out Of Your Comfort Zone

We sometimes need to do things that are different, new, and often uncomfortable. Perhaps we have done things the same way and feel comfortable or are afraid to learn or try something new. Like learning to embrace change, trying things that are new and often uncomfortable, brings excitement to what otherwise has become predictable and stagnant. It also provides a way for us to grow by giving us confidence from accomplishing something we weren't sure we could do.

Another way to add excitement and energy to your life is by continually challenging yourself. Look for things you have wanted to try or things that you have wanted to pursue more in-depth or with more focus. You now have the time to pursue many of these activities and/or passions.

Are you willing to get out of your comfort zone? Are you continuing to challenge yourself in the areas you want to learn more about?

Seek Guidance When Needed

Making the transition into retirement can be a challenging time, fraught with questions, concerns, fears and stress. Talk with friends or former colleagues who have previously retired to hear their thoughts, feelings, and support. Listen to how they have handled the transition, and what worked and didn't work for them. Find out what they would do differently.

You can also hire a retirement coach to guide you through the challenges and options in retirement and can provide the needed assistance for making a successful transition into retirement. Sharing your questions and struggles with someone who understands these challenges can help get you back on the path to a confident and happy retirement.

Do you have someone who can provide support and guidance during your retirement transition?

Why It Is Important To Develop Resilience

Retirement is a time of great transition and a new phase in our life. It is a time to look toward the future with excitement and energy and not a time to dread or fear. As we discovered previously, retirement offers challenges that are unique to this time. As a result, it is important to develop resiliency and apply the ways presented to deal with this adversity — whether the challenge is physical, mental, social or spiritual.

Developing resiliency is important prior to and into retirement. By developing resiliency in retirement, we not only prepare ourselves to handle challenges and setbacks, but we also can keep the challenges from affecting us.

Resilience is important for moving forward when challenged by either the financial or non-financial aspects that confront us approaching retirement and as we settle into retirement. The non-financial aspects of retirement can be categorized as the mental, physical, social, and spiritual areas of our life.

As you approach and decide to enter retirement, make a conscious effort to practice and learn resilience. Look at situations that provide challenges and use the methods of coping with challenges as ways to develop your resilience. Life in retirement has a lot to offer. We have come too far not to live the life we have envisioned in retirement.

About The Author

Reid Stone has over 20 years of experience in the wealth management industry, primarily leading operations, technology, and project management for a variety of financial advisory businesses. From this background, he observed that planning for retirement is focused on one thing, how much a person has accumulated for retirement. There is little or no focus on preparing people for the non-financial aspects of retirement. This experience led him to start My Life's Encore (www.MyLifesEncore.com). Reid holds an MBA from Minnesota State University, Mankato. He is a Certified Professional Retirement Coach and a board member of the Retirement Coaches Association.

Notes

1. Sheryl Sandberg and Adam Grant, *Option B: Facing Adversity, Building Resilience and Finding Joy* (New York: Alfred A. Knopf, 2017).

2. Steve Maraboli, *Life, the Truth, and Being Free* (New York: A Better Today Publishing, 2009).

3. Lynda Gratton and Andrew Scott, *The 100 Year Life — Living and Working in an Age of Longevity* (London; New York: Bloomsbury Business, 2017).

4. William Bridges, *Transitions — Making Sense of Life's Changes* (Massachusetts: Da Capo Lifelong Books, 2004).

Inward/Outward Journey: Doing The Work To Find Your Passion

By Rita Gallagher

Who are you? I don't mean, "What is your profession?" or "Are you a mom or dad, husband or wife, sister, or brother?" I mean, "Who are you?"

I have another question for you: What are you called to do? Are these questions easy for you to answer?

"Mister" Fred Rogers said, "Choices come from a deep sense of who you are." So, if you know who you are, then it will be easy to answer the question, "What are you called to do?"

This chapter will help you answer both questions so that as you transition into the best, most exciting period of your life, you will be better prepared to embrace it, enjoy it, and live it to your fullest potential!

So, let's get to that question of "Who are you?" How often have you thought about it? We typically identify ourselves by what we do. Or more often, we identify ourselves as a mother, father, wife, husband, married, single, female, or male. After we get past all that, then what?

When I was posed with this question, I have to admit, I wasn't sure what to say. I started out with, "OK, I'm a mom, a good friend, a reliable sister, team player at work, and easy to get along with." But that didn't really sound like who I was deep down inside. There must be more.

Mark Twain said, "The two most important days of your life are the day you are born and the day you find out why."

I believe that once you discover the "why," what you are called to do will show up.

Let's start our Inward Journey by identifying what we are passionate about or what inspires us. In Wayne Dyer's *Living an Inspired Life*, he talks about the difference between motivation and inspiration. He says, if motivation is grabbing an idea and carrying it through to completion, then inspiration is the reverse. He says, inspiration is when an idea has taken hold of us from the invisible reality of Spirit.

Being in-Spirit is the place where we connect to the invisible reality that ultimately leads us to our calling. These callings pull us toward them and keep appearing in our consciousness.[1]

The exercise below will help you get more in tune with who you are. It helps craft words that better describe our essence. Or, as mentioned above, what inspires us.

There are several ways to discover what you are passionate about — what inspires you. Below is a list of questions to ask yourself to start the juices flowing:

- What opens your heart?

- What inspires you?

- What makes you come alive?

- What are you doing when you are totally lost in the moment?

- How do you feel when you hear a song that touches your soul?

- What are you doing when you are in 'the zone'?

- What comes easy for you?

- What makes you joyful?

- What makes you feel good?

- Where is your happy place?

- What can you never get enough of (besides chocolate)?

- What makes you cry when you are happy?

- How do you feel when you are in nature?

- What are you doing when you lose yourself in anything that brings you peace?

- What do you love to do?

- What are you grateful for?

- How do you feel when you are in the moment and really know it?

Discovering the answers to some of these questions should bring you closer to learning who you really are. You might consider asking a close friend or family member. You may also try meditating or yoga to help you slow down and use your breath to find inner peace and reflection. Prayer is another way to get centered.

Chip Gaines, from the TV show, *Fixer Upper*, in his book, *Capital Gaines*,[2] says, "We were created to live passionately — all of us, no matter our personality type or circumstances. The human heart was made to swell and jump and stir; that's a fact. It took me a while to figure out what makes my heart feel that way. But this is perhaps one of the most crucial things to know about ourselves."

Living passionately means knowing your purpose and focusing your time and energy on that purpose. It's doing what makes you feel alive and gives your life meaning.

The next question is this: How are you showing up in life? Are you living intentionally? Living intentionally begs you to be in the present moment. Being present, or mindful takes effort. With all the distractions and busyness of life, being in the moment is difficult. It takes conscious effort and a lot of practice.

"Realize deeply that the present moment is all you ever have."

— Eckhart Tolle

Dyer, in his *Change Your Thoughts — Change Your Life*[3] live seminar, says there are four things to focus on when we want to get in touch with ourselves and truly let go and let God.

First, he talks about moving away from fear to being curious. He says, when we are curious it allows us to be adventuresome. Look at your curiosity as a learning experience — something new to create harmony within your life.

Second, he talks about moving from attachment to letting go. One of his popular quotes is, "Have a mind that is open to everything and attached to nothing." Think about the things we are attached to — our jobs, our house, our car, our children, our stuff, etc. There are some really good books out there that talk about the more we get rid of our stuff, the better we feel. It actually frees our souls — unclutters us physically and spiritually!

Third, is moving from being in control to trust. He says that with this awareness, this trusting in a higher power, you really control nothing. Go with the flow and live in the moment. Let go and let God.

The last thing he mentions is going from entitlement to humility. When we give up entitlement, we give up the ego. The ego is what always gets in our way. When we move to humility, we put others first.

This Inward Journey is a very pers
journey you must spend time with. (
that allows you to contemplate some
questions above. Bring a journal and
your feelings and thoughts. Take your
be worth it!

Before
us fr

Here is a great exercise that may help yo. ...scover
what you are passionate about. It is adapted from
the book, The Two Most Important Days — How to
Find Your Purpose and Live a Happier, Healthier
Life, by Sanjiv Chopra and Gina Vild. I highly
recommend the book.

- You will need thirty 3-inch by 5-inch note
  cards.

- Every day, for the next 30 days, write down
  five to seven things you did that day.

- Next, rate each activity on a scale of 1-10
  based on how much you enjoyed the
  experience, with 10 being amazing.

- After 30 days, cross out all the activities that
  were a six or below.

What you have left should give you some insights as
to where you should be focusing your time and
energy.

Now that you have an idea of what makes your heart
sing, it's time to take some action.

e go there, let's take a look at what keeps ...m taking action. Fear is one thing that keeps ...s from taking action — probably more often than we want to admit. I read somewhere recently, once we get past the fear, life is a fantastic journey! Remember the saying "no risk, no reward"? There is a lot of truth to that adage. It's easy to be complacent, to get into a routine, or to play it safe. Time just kind of slips by and we are in the same place we were last year, and the year before, and so on.

Here's the good news! Once you do the work with your Inward Journey — once you find your passion and discover why you are here — my hope is you will be excited and motivated to get to work. Don't let fear hold you back. So, what if you make some mistakes, or things don't go as planned the first time you take action. Take a step back, discover the lesson learned, and try again.

Something else to consider: How are you looking at things? Are you skeptical? Are you not a risk taker? Is playing it safe easier? Have others discouraged you from your dreams? Does that inner voice talk you out of things? Don't let the voice in your head defeat your passion or enthusiasm. Be enthusiastic about your passion and your purpose. Dyer talks about being enthusiastic about all that you do. He says, to have that passion with enthusiasm literally means "the God (*enthos*) within (*iasm*)." The God inside of you is telling you to take the risk and follow your passion. What have you got to lose?

Now, let's get busy. So, what does this Outward Journey path look like? Let's break it down into three main categories:

1. Primary Relationships

2. Work

3. Community

Primary Relationships

These are where so much of who we are or how we think of ourselves were established. Other relationships affect us, but not as much as our primary ones. Having good relationships is one of the keys to longevity. Now, listen closely: The important word here is "good." Good relationships keep us happier and healthier, based on the Harvard Grant Study.[4] Their studies have shown that trusted relationships can even protect our brains from cognitive decline. The opposite to having good relationships results in loneliness, which is toxic and typically leads to depression. From the book, *The Two Most Important Days*,[5] "the study found that it's not the number of friends you have at age 50 but the quality of relationships that matter. In fact, your satisfaction with relationships at 50 is more important than your cholesterol levels as a determinant of health and happiness three decades later at age 80!"[4]

What do your important relationships look like right now? Do they need some work?

Work

This is another area to consider. Will you work during retirement? If so, will it be full time or part time? Will you start a business or maybe do volunteer work? What are your vocational priorities at this time of your life?

Community

This can involve many things. It can be big or small. How involved do you want to be? Being involved with others gives us a sense of self-worth and meaning of its own. Ask yourself, who can walk alongside you.

Life is a gift. Sometimes, an outward journey can be as simple as greeting the day with an open heart. A grateful attitude is a wonderful way to begin the day. Take a few minutes before you get busy with all the things you need to do and take time to reflect on being thankful for the day.

I recently attended a presentation by Ben Nemtin, who co-wrote the book, *What Do You Want To Do Before You Die?*[6] Ben, two brothers who lived next-door, and another friend were at their wits end, just out of college, trying to figure out where to go and what to do with their lives.

They asked each other, "If anything were possible, what do you want to do before you die?" They eventually decided to write down a list of 100 things they wanted to do before they die, and to help and encourage others to do the same.

They bought on old van and headed out together to work on their list. They also decided that each time they completed something on their list and were able to cross it off, they would help someone else, usually a total stranger, cross something off their list. It was their way of giving back. Nothing was considered out of reach.

More than 10 years later, they have accomplished many things on their list, a few of which are: Learn to fly, pay for someone's groceries, play basketball with the president of the United States, and make a music video.

From Nemtin's presentation, here are some important points I wrote down on how to help you succeed with your list:

- What's important? This is the question we have been working on with our Inward Journey. As mentioned before, this takes some time to think, pray, and meditate about.

- Write it down. When we write things down, they become real. Now, we have something to reflect back on. Nemtin equates it to going from a dream to something tangible.

- Talk about it. Share your list. Tell someone whom you trust the things you want to accomplish before you die. Maybe it's a significant other, good friend, or sibling. Better yet, ask that person if they would like to share with you what they would like to accomplish and you can hold each other accountable. As a bonus, there may be a few things on both of your lists that are the same, and you could do them together!

- Be persistent. Don't give up. Be determined to be successful. This will definitely increase your odds of success!

- Take "Moonshots." Go for something that is out of your comfort zone. Most people don't take the big risks. What's holding you back? Big goals are motivating!

- Help others. Give back. Whether it is helping them achieve their own dream or just doing some volunteer work. How about just paying something forward?

In writing this book, Nemtin and his friends said, "We hope that the dreams and words filling these pages will ignite part of you and halt you long enough to sincerely think about what is important to you. It's easy to think about what's important to others but rarely do we truly listen to our gut and our heart, and that is where a bucket list should grow. If nothing in the world were impossible, what would you do? Even if it is impossible, what do you want to do before you die?" [6]

Maybe this would be a perfect time to do a little reflecting and write down the things you still want to accomplish.

Now that you are winding down your career, or maybe already out of the job market, what is holding you back? Have some fun and adventure and at the same time give back to those you can help. It's a "win-win" no matter what!

I found a poem many years ago called *The Dash* that I have often read at workshops where we talk about what our stories are. We write down our 'Old Story', the one that keeps us stuck with all kinds of excuses for not being the person we truly are. The group does a lot of self-reflection on their own, similar to what I have suggested in this chapter. We then tear up the Old Story and write our New Story. Our New Story is what we are going to do going forward in order to be the person we truly are. I read this poem at Retirement workshops now to help inspire those of us entering this grand chapter of our lives called retirement.

The poem, *The Dash*, talks about a man reading a eulogy at a friend's funeral, speaking of the dates on her tombstone. He talks about how the most important of these two dates between her birth and death was the dash between the years. The point of the poem is to exam how you live your dash and what is most important to you. I highly recommend you take a minute to look up and read this poem: *The Dash*, by Linda Ellis (Copyright Inspire Kindness, LLC 1996, www.thedashpoem.com).

So how are you living your dash right now? What's holding you back? Get busy. Write it down. Make it happen!

Remember this, the world is wide open for you to follow your dreams and accomplish things you still want to do. Believe that *everything* is possible.

My wish is that you find your passion, inspiration and purpose and make the rest of your life the best journey yet!

> *Yesterday, I was clever and wanted to change the world. Today, I am wise, so I am changing myself.*

— RUMI

Special thanks to Pastor Kai Nilsen and Kevin Ryan for their spiritual teachings and guidance.

About The Author

Rita Gallagher works at Nationwide Financial in Columbus, Ohio and has been responsible for building and sustaining their current coaching culture. She also facilitated training programs around coaching competencies and energy management. Prior to joining Nationwide in 2007, Rita was a HR Director and has over 20 years of experience in the HR profession. Rita received her MBA as well as her Graduate Coaching certification from Franklin University, Columbus, Ohio. She is a Certified Business Coach through World Association of Business Coaches as well as a Certified Retirement Coach through Retirement Coaching Options. She can be contacted at ritagall514@gmail.com

Notes

1. Wayne W. Dyer, *Living an Inspired Life: Your Ultimate Calling* (Carlsbad, CA: Hay House, 2016).

2. Chip Gaines, *Capital Gaines: Smart Things I Learned Doing Stupid Stuff* (Nashville, TN: Thomas Nelson, 2018).

3. *The Change Your Thoughts — Change Your Life Live Seminar,* Wayne Dyer (Hay House, 2009), DVD.

4. Alvin Powell, "Decoding Keys to a Heathy Life," *Harvard Gazette*, February 2, 2012.

5. Sanjiv Chopra and Gina Vild, *The Two Most Important Days: How to Find Your Purpose and Live a Happier, Healthier Life* (Sydney, N.S.W.: Hachette Australia, 2018), and Robert Waldinger, 2015, *What Makes a Good Life? Lessons from the Longest Study on Happiness* [video], https://www.ted.com/talks/robert_waldinger_w hat_makes_a_good_life_lessons_from_the_lo ngest_study_on_happiness/up-next.

6. Ben Nemtin et al., *What Do You Want to Do before You Die?: Moving, Unexpected, and Inspiring Answers to Life's Most Important Question* (New York: Artisan, 2018), and Ben Nemtin, 2015, *Six Steps to Crossing Anything Off Your Bucket List,*

117

https://www.youtube.com/watch?v=H6Y7mfxE
aco

Ted Talks

The Game That Can Give You 10 Extra Years of Life, by Jane McGonigal, 2012

Moving Toward A Fulfilling Retirement

By David Dinsmore

Whether you consider yourself well-equipped to face retirement or are scratching and clawing for opportunities for a more successful retirement, I want to share with you that transitions are for moving through not for camping out.

The late William Bridges, an expert in the field of personal and work transitions, explains that transition isn't just a change as a result of an external circumstance. Transition is the inner process people go through to deal with the change, as they let go of how things used to be and orient themselves to life as it is now.

Moving through transitions involves four steps:

1. Awareness of where one is in the moment

2. What the limiting thoughts are that are keeping one stuck

3. What one receives as a benefit for remaining stuck

4. Allowing new energy and *hope* to enter one's life from the greatest gift we have, which is our health

In our limited time together, I would like to show you three ways that give you access to moving through periods of feeling stagnant in your life.

The Dream Development Cycle ®

How do we manage uncertainty and change in our lives? Let us use a model to help us become more aware of where one is in the retirement stage of life. This model has been very helpful for me, personally, during the sale of my first business many years ago. During and after selling my business, I wrestled with what life is or would be like, no longer being a dentist. I have experienced firsthand the power an identity can hold over us.

We all have invisible rules we enforce on ourselves about how life should be. I discovered this model many years ago from observation and considerable reflection. You may notice something similar in our own life. This model is divided into four stages. It is circular in form and I will describe the model as if you are looking at the face of a clock, beginning with stage 1.

As we move through this model of change, I invite you to ask yourself which stage you are in.

Stage 1: The 'Preparation' Stage (6-9 o'clock)

Stage 1 is commonly centered on the stage of "leaving home" for the first time. It is usually marked by an "idea." An idea to do something, become someone, or move away from something or someone. This is the very tiniest, micro-beginning stage of action towards one's dream or deepest desire. A dream is most characterized, in its infancy, by a powerful, almost automatic pull towards something such as a vision or a person. It can also

120

be a move away from a hurt, pain or from a troubled environment, situation or person.

This stage is marked by considerable learning. This stage is further characterized by naïve optimism, lightness of being, joy, trust, searching, exploration of options, play and creativity, passion, a sense of timelessness, yearning, being accident prone, being funny and silly, learning about relationships, and gaining an occupational identity.

Identity is the key word here. For men especially, the word identity can potentially carry a lot of weight. We will look at this more in the mini-transition phase below. Stage 1 can be viewed as a "holding tank," with the main purpose of this stage being growth and preparation. A good example of this phase is someone about to start college, vocational school, or the military.

For those in retirement: This stage is when long-awaited travel and adventures can take place. This is the time to dream again and make plans. How about creating a bucket list or a discovery list for the next five years? What would you like to learn or do? Would you like to learn a new language or take up dancing? Would you like to write a book or your memoirs to record your great experiences? Is there a new business you would like to pursue?

Stage 2: The "Performance" Phase (9-1 o'clock)

This is where you find your fit, make your mark and begin to form your identity of who you are in the world. For many, this is the stage that follows college or the military. This is the time when you "live the dream." Stage 2 is characterized by confidence, courage, energy, alignment with the world, collaboration, competitiveness, goals, risk taking, commitment, and optimism.

It is here that we actually "do" what we have been preparing for. As a society, we are most familiar with this stage of life. This is the stage we build our lives around, the time when we implement things like time management systems, debriefing strategies and goal setting or talk about work in depth with friends.

For those in retirement: This could be a time to embark on entrepreneurship.

With regard to a new business after 50:

- Studies are showing that there is more innovation in business from those over 50 than those in their 20s. Of course, you knew this!

- You own your age, your strengths and experience

- You benefit from a large list of contacts

- You can direct your life's work to contribution and service

People love this stage and think that it will just keep getting better and last forever. This is the most stable, predictable, and challenging of the four stages. However, even if we are successful at reaching our goals, we can get out of sync and become low on energy and reactive. The challenges wane, the routines become familiar, and you feel imprisoned by the very scenario you thought would lead to fulfillment. You then can experience early stages of burnout. Perhaps you may be familiar with this concept.

Stage 3: The 'Stagnation' Stage (1-3 o'clock)

This stage begins as a low grade burnout or apathy that begins to become more prevalent with each passing week. It can later transition to a despondency (a deep spiritual lethargy). Stage 3 is characterized by fear, anger, sadness, irritability, helplessness, hopelessness, cynicism, low energy, seemingly no alternatives, an unwillingness to change or move ahead, reactivity, denial, or simply boredom, a sense of "is this all there is?," or a feeling that you don't belong here anymore.

Stage 3 is a down time, a protracted sense of decline when you are not happy with your life, but you don't think you can do much about it. You try to hang on to where you are, but your enjoyment and passion decreases with each passing day.

For those in retirement: This is the stage that author and entrepreneur Robert Laura writes about in his book, *The Dark Side of Retirement*.[1]

I mentioned that everyone wants to be in Stage 2. However, most people are actually in Stage 3. This is where "misery loves company."

How does one get out of Stage 3? Well, there are two ways.

One is called a mini-career/vocation/life transition. You attempt to change the external environment by moving, accepting a job transfer, getting more education, or even getting a divorce (though not a good idea). You attempt to do anything that energizes you or feels appropriate that can inject new life into you and allows you to move back into Stage 2.

For those in retirement: This can occur mostly with relationships with loved ones. If a relationship is not working you may not get positive results despite your best efforts. This is because, even though your intention is well-meaning, you are simply trying the same things over and over with a focus that doesn't change.

The second way to move from Stage 3 is marked by internal change and emotion. This marks the end of a stage and life as you knew it before. Even though life in Stage 3 was not great, you were fairly content there because it was familiar and you knew who you were as a person and what to expect on a day-to-day basis. The important thing to note here is that this change can be felt very deeply, like a loss or a mini-death.

For those in retirement: This is perhaps the No. 1 challenge in retirement.

The reason that many people, more specifically men, struggle with personal identity is that they merge who they are as a person with the career role in life that they have been playing for so many years. Therefore, when this role is no longer played there is a heavy sense of loss in the person's life.

As we enter into Stage 4, there is a cleansing of the self that you once knew for a new identity and sense of self.

Stage 4: The 'Land of the Spirit' Stage (3-6 o'clock)

After many years or even decades of living and focusing on life outside of ourselves, there is an awakening to an entire new world inside.

This is the search for the Inner Self. The commonly accepted term for this stage is a "sabbatical." Our culture accepts the term "sabbatical," but the two terms are not necessarily the same. The characteristics of this stage are grief, sadness, feeling like you are in limbo and lost. Once these emotions are worked through, the other side brings liberation, relief, quiet excitement, a new beginning, inner confidence, finding an inner voice, spiritual discovery, and the courage to simply "be" who you were meant to be.

The Land of the Spirit is a detachment from the life stage that wasn't working any longer — taking an emotional time out to heal, reflect, and discover new directions to your life. An intention to do so can lead to renewal and a new sense of purpose. This is the land of being and silence — not action. People in this stage are quiet, withdrawn, and can be unsure of themselves. It is often considered un-American to be in this stage as there is no direct cultural reward.

For those in retirement: This is an understandably difficult yet very valuable place to be. Our life energy is dynamic and always moving. If we reject this invitation of movement, our lives can become stuck, stagnant, lonely and depression can set in quickly.

Don't necessarily think of Stage 4 as a linear next step in the progression of life. It actually overlays all of the stages and has been present all the time. It just gets pushed away for many of us because of our hurry or necessity to form our identity and get plugged in to the world. It then becomes a way of life.

Ceremony

You may be entering retirement directly from the powerful Stage 2 or maybe you have been limping along for a few years in Stage 3. You might have been in Stage 1 getting ready for retirement with purpose, excitement, and energy.

In either case, the retirement stage is best entered into with a type of ceremony that is felt deeply.

On one hand, it can be very celebratory with a spirit of gratitude for the people and opportunities in your life. It is important to acknowledge yourself for the gifts you have received, the people you have served, and the accomplishments you have made. This is a celebration.

On the other hand, there may be a part of you that needs to go through a mini-death of sorts. Please allow that to happen with the aid of this book, a friend, or coach. Many times, just knowing that this is a possible outcome can be a big help. I call that awareness. We can never have enough awareness in our lives. Remember, you are retiring from a role — not from your life. You are still a full, living being full of spirit, hopes, and dreams. Bring on the next chapter of contribution!

Move Your Body

A second way to move through a stagnant phase of life is to move your body. Movement is key, for both your body and your thoughts. Picture in your mind a circle. Now take out a piece of paper and write at the top of the circle, or the 12:00 position the words "Current Thoughts." At the 8:00 position place the word "Body." At the 4:00 position the words, "Spoken Words." Now, place the word "Emotions" in the middle of the circle.

During any given mood or physiological state, this circle will be a composite of what is going on inside your thought mechanisms, or soul. Our soul consists of our mind, thoughts, emotions and the core of our soul — our heart. Thoughts lead the way. If I am joyful, my body (on the lower left) will act, behave, move, or hold itself in a joyful posture or feeling. If I am sad, discouraged, or stuck, my body will likewise behave and position itself in a disappointed, stuck, or closed and downtrodden way. Continuing with our model, the words we speak will be shaped by the framework of the emotions and thoughts that come from our circle.

Though there are many ways to change this physiologic state, I will address two.

If you are stuck in a low, despondent emotional state, recognize it as an alarm or a signal that you are associating a thought that is literally throwing or propelling you into an emotion. This can lead your body into feeling stuck and you will therefore speak words that come from this emotional state, resulting in disempowering language.

Body

First, let's move our body. Strength training, or at least some sort of resistance training (movement with a touch of weight or resistance to make the movement more challenging) over the age of 50 is critical. It can help conditions such as arthritis, diabetes, osteoporosis, obesity, back pain, and even depression (a Stage 3 emotion).

Resistance training, even just utilizing your body weight, helps to build and maintain muscle mass. The University of Pittsburgh conducted a study, in 2011, of high-level recreational athletes aged 40-81. They observed and tested these recreational athletes over a broad range of muscle group tests, body mass testing and adipose/fat percentage. They found that the subjects could retain the same levels of lean muscle mass from their 40s on into their 80s![2] This is a counterintuitive study from what was previously thought. The Pittsburgh study showed that strength was maintained, as well. Please note, however, that other similar studies show that, even though muscle mass can be maintained, corresponding strength does decrease. I think this is because the Pittsburgh study included subjects who were athletes and have benefited from years of neuromuscular pathways that have been well trained.

If anything, this should invite us to move now, not tomorrow! At the time of this writing, I am 58 years old and have performed at a high level all my life and although my muscle mass is maintained, my strength has indeed decreased. In either case, it is worth moving and challenging your body for maximum anti-aging benefits.

Challenging and moving your body is a great way to feel alive! If you are well versed in exercise, head to the gym or outside with your spouse or your friends and get moving. If you are a beginner or an intermediate exerciser, I strongly recommend you work on becoming body aware. This increases your proprioceptive awareness of your body (awareness of where your body, head, and arms are without looking). If you are new, let's begin with the following movements.

Vertical Movement

While at the gym, look for a TRX strap hanging from a high bar. If the gym doesn't have one you can simply hold on to a nearby bar that is a bit higher than your movement with one hand to perform the following exercise. You many also use a doorjamb inside of your room to support your weight and spot your efforts.

We will be doing a modified supported squat. As we get older, it is critical to maintain range of motion as much as possible. I am not concerned with weight or resistance during this exercise. You have met the objective if you are able to maintain flexibility and range of motion. Place your feet shoulder width apart and parallel. Hold on to your support and simply lower your body, allowing your hips to fold, then your knees to bend, as you approach 90 degrees of knee bend. If this is too much, simply squat as low as you can without sharp pain. Keep your shoulders back and focus on the hip and knee bend. Make sure to keep your knees behind your angles. Four to five sets of eight repetitions is a great place to work toward. Our joints can handle the movement, just go slowly. Our joints fail from misalignment of our body and poor posture, not specifically from age.

Horizontal Movement

For the next exercise lay on your belly. Spread your arms horizontally like you are Superman/woman. Tuck your belly in and your shoulder blades together, and raise your upper body off the floor about 1-3 inches. Hold for four seconds and lower down. Repeat this exercise 10 times. Try again, this time raising your legs at the same time as your upper body. Do this for 10 repetitions of four seconds each.

Body Awareness

Next, sit in a chair with the back against the wall. Take in a deep breath, close your eyes, and visualize the movement. With your neck lifted long and tall, let your arms fall against the side of the chair alongside your waist. Slowly raise your left arm (keeping it straight) to shoulder width and lower it. Repeat with the right arm. Repeat this movement with both arms moving very slowly maintaining the length of your neck. Each repetition should take about six seconds. Repeat this movement eight times.

While sitting on the chair, move on to the next exercise. Keeping both hips on the chair, gently raise your left knee up about 1-2 inches above the chair. Hold it there and slowly lower it down. Do this exercise eight times and repeat for the right leg.

Work toward being able to stand against the wall while performing this exercise over the next couple of weeks. Stand with your feet close together, about six inches away from the wall and work to have your hips, back, and head against the wall. Close your eyes, visualize, and feel where your neck and hips are during this position.

Movement Through Your Feet

Healthy feet provide energy to your entire body. This is the next level of difficulty. Support yourself next to a doorjamb or wall. Face straight ahead with your feet as close to each other as possible while still feeling balanced and comfortable. Place your arms at your waist and raise your heels off the ground as high as they can go. We are working for time; hold this position as long as you can. Begin with five sets of 10 seconds and increase the time as you are able.

To make the movement more advanced, raise your hands to shoulder height. In the next few days, raise them to the sky in a celebratory pose and hold your heels off the ground. For more of a challenge, close your eyes! Be sure you are next to the door jam or wall for support when you do that, though. This move will greatly increase your balance and proprioception as well as your feet, leg, and core strength.

Focus your awareness, first on your feet against the floor. This is your root and grounding. Then allow your awareness to come to your hips and quickly back to the feet. Spot yourself and watch your balance improve with 60 seconds every day!

For those of you that want more intensity, simply add more resistance or time to the movements.

Walking

Now, let's make it even easier by walking. Multiple short bouts of walking have been shown to encourage those who don't traditionally enjoy exercise. The movements we have been discussing fall into that category and offer even an added benefit. Taking a 15-minute walk three times per day following meals has been shown to have a positive effect on blood sugar levels.[3] A similar idea has even been called "exercise snacking."[4] What an easy concept to remember! Can you invite your spouse or grandchildren to join you? We have heard that our metabolism slows down when we age. This is true, but if we stay active — moving as has been mentioned — our metabolism will be regulated by the musculoskeletal system demands placed on it.

Other wonderful movement options include yoga, swimming pool exercises, the Alexander technique, Feldenkrais, dance and (my favorite) Pilates.

Movement of Thoughts

Our third and final movement is to become aware of our thoughts which places us at the 12:00 position of our circle. Holding your thoughts in or withdrawing your emotions is death to the movement of life. With regard to relationships, create intentional quality time with your spouse that allows for open and frequent conversation. Make time to stay in close contact with friends.

Prayer

Prayer is another relationship. By nature, prayer is a dialogue. It is a reconciliation or union with God. Above, I mentioned hope is a gift and gives us great energy. Hope is a vital part of prayer and is intimately associated with love. Hope is the power behind love and is what causes us to look forward to the reward of love. Love arrives through the pathway of hope.

A critical aspect of prayer is to allow all of your awareness to focus in on your heart. As you begin in prayer allow the thinking part of yourself to descend into your heart area. One way to begin this is to inhale into your heart and then visualize an ocean wave taking away your thoughts, or have them fly right over you without landing on or in you. Continually breathe into your heart and focus on your breath. Feel free to bring your faith tradition into this prayer. For Christians, it could be a favorite or needed verse or prayer like "Lord Jesus Christ, have mercy on me." Slowly focus on each word, allowing each to center deep inside you. Be slow, quiet, and patient as comfort, hope, peace, and gratitude come over you. Then allow even the words to drift away.

About The Author

"Many influencers and leaders are on a journey of discovery. But oftentimes their pain has them stuck. I help them break through to achieve their next level."

A loving husband and dad, a long time dentist and dental entrepreneur, a student of life, a stand for human potential and love; a former college football player/high school coach, life and performance coach to professionals, PGA teaching professionals, an NFL quarterback and coach, marriage facilitation trainer, former personal trainer and holder of numerous full body sports medicine, life coaching, chronic pain and neurophysiology certifications. MA Christian Apologetics. Visit DavidDinsmore.com

Notes

1. Robert Laura, *The Dark Side of Retirement* (Brighton, MI: The Retirement Project, 2011).

2. Andrew P. Wroblewski et al., "Chronic Exercise Preserves Lean Muscle Mass in Masters Athletes," *The Physician and Sportsmedicine* 39, no. 3 (2011), doi:10.3810/psm.2011.09.1933.

3. Loretta DiPietro, Andrei Gribok, Michelle S. Stevens, Larry F. Hamm, William Rumpler. Three 15-min Bouts of Moderate Postmeal Walking Significantly Improves 24-h Glycemic Control in Older People at Risk for Impaired Glucose Tolerance. Diabetes Care Oct 2013, 36 (10) 3262-3268; DOI: 10.2337/dc13-0084

4. Francois ME, Baldi JC, Manning PJ, Lucas SJ, Hawley JA, Williams MJ, Cotter JD. 'Exercise snacks' before meals: a novel strategy to improve glycemic control in individuals with insulin resistance. Diabetologia. 2014 Jul;57(7):1437-45. doi: 10.1007/s00125-014-3244-6. Epub 2014 May 10

Mates: Don't Retire Without Them

By Joel Shuflin

To get this far in life, you needed them. To live the second half of life richly, you need them even more.

Mates. Depending on who you ask, and perhaps what country you live in, they are: The disappearing second sock, classmates we haven't seen in decades, soulmates with whom we may or may not cohabit, or people we make (made) babies with. In Australia, they're the guys and gals we hang out with at the bar.

Three Reasons You Need Mates

But let's go back to that first statement: "To live the second half of life richly, you need them even more."

Why?

First, because you'll live healthier. "Social relationships, or the relative lack thereof, constitute a major risk factor for health—rivaling the effect of well-established health risk factors such as cigarette smoking, blood pressure, blood lipids, obesity and physical activity."[1]

There are dozens of public health studies and research into the psychology of support systems over the past three decades that overwhelmingly conclude that those individuals who are isolated have failing health and die sooner than those with social groups and support.

Second, you'll learn more. Continuing to learn is not only good for the health of your brain, it's good for you sense of contentment. Social learning theorist Albert Bandura demonstrated over and over that learning from others is primary for all of us (just think back to how you learned to play video games, poker, or charades).

Learning by modeling others' behavior and skills isn't the only way mates help us learn — they also can challenge and extend our thinking about the world around us. More on this later, but this is one reason why we need a variety of mates in our lives.

Third, mates hold you accountable. "Whoa!" I hear you saying. Before you go down that line of thought — I'm NOT talking about people being "in your business." I am talking about the benefit of having people expect something from you. Your mates will expect you to be you, to be consistent with the person they know you to be.

Admittedly, you could have them totally believing you're someone or something that you're not. Whatever persona you project to your mates, they'll expect that — and that expectation creates an accountability for you to be consistent.

This means of course, you need to show up authentically, because the real value of accountability is when people hold you accountable to be the person that you truly want to be. Since we're talking about the second half of life, the age-old question of, "What do you want them to write on your tombstone?" feels even more relevant. If you're not certain of the answer to that yet, a good coach can help you think it through until you discover the answer.

The Three Kinds of Mates You Need

There are three kinds of mates that I believe have been essential in your journey throughout life, and you'll need these three kinds of mates even more as you move into the second half of life: cohorts, collaborators, and co-creators.

Cohorts

Remember elementary school? I remember mine well. The school building was long and white with green trimmed windows. Huge areas of grass surrounded the blacktop playground on which there were painted lines for hop-scotch, four square, basketball and to delineate the "don't-go-there-that's-fifth-and-sixth-grade-only" territory.

And although I haven't seen them in half a century, I still remember the names of my elementary school mates: Ricky, Lyle, Dana (the brainy girl who could also outrun most of us), and of course Walter, whom everyone knew only by his nickname, "Ears."

We were inseparable from Kindergarten on. We were on the foursquare court together at recess. We chased the girls together, taunting them with single-serve potato chip bags buzzing with captured bees. We raced each other to complete in-class assignments and to be the fastest in our speed-reading sessions.

The four of us were top students. Every year, without fail, whether we were in the same classroom, we all were in the finals for the grade-level spelling contest.

Interestingly, though, we never saw each other much once the final bell rang at the end of the school day. Sure, once in a great while I'd see "Ears" at church. There was one summer when I would often be at Ricky's house begging to read his (now very valuable) pristine, plastic-wrapped collection of Marvel and D.C. comics.

For the most part, however, there was an entirely different set of people I interacted with after school — those who lived on my block or, on Sunday, those I saw at church. That group was a totally separate circle: Mike, Paul, Sandy, Cherry, and Leslie.

At the end of sixth grade, I moved far enough away that I would not be seeing these classmates ever again.

We were friends, for sure. Yet we only really came together when we were called together by the legal requirement for us to be in school, and grouped together by the results of some aptitude test. We were a cohort.

A cohort, in the usual sense, is a group of people that are brought together by someone else for a specific, and often limited, purpose. A cohort could be a group of students going through a program of study together. It could be a group of subjects that are lumped together by a researcher.

Throughout life, chances are you've been in all kinds of cohorts at school, at work, and in your community. It's that cross-departmental team your boss assigned you to work on, the committee the civic club asked you to chair, those three people the tee master assigned you to play golf with to make up a foursome.

Don't think that cohorts are a throw-away group that you don't have to invest in. They're not. In fact, I believe cohorts are vitally important to your successful and satisfying life after 50.

Here's why: Cohorts give us an identity within a group. From "I'm in Mrs. Brown's second grade class," to "I'm part of the employee feedback committee at MicroTec," we've been part of cohorts. Those cohorts contribute to our identity within the community and our well-being.[2]

In most retirement scenarios, leaving an employer or stepping down as a business owner immediately takes us out of many of our cohorts — the people in our department, the people at our bus or train stop, the business networking group, the franchisee support group.

While we are working at our job or on our business, we have cohorts created for us. In the second half of life, especially after employment, we need to choose cohorts to associate with.

"I've a circle of close friends. Isn't that enough?"

No.

Here's the big reason it isn't: Cohorts, by definition, are groups that are created for us. Although you can choose to join or not join a cohort, the composition of the cohort usually isn't up to you.

You've been brought together by someone else, and that means you're going to be in a cohort with diverse people — you will encounter divergent opinions, conflicting values, and upside down (from your perspective, anyway) ways of thinking.

Frankly, that's wonderful! I believe that one of the greatest risks of retirement is that we can easily stop interacting with people who are not like us.

As we continue to encounter this kind of diversity of people in life, we will have the opportunity to continue to examine our own values, prejudices, foregone conclusions, and paradigms. In short, we increase our opportunity to grow. All three of the benefits of mates can be found in some degree within a cohort.

One final question about cohorts seems obvious to me: Is the need to be part of a cohort and extrovert-only thing? I readily admit I am an extrovert, so I've put that question to about a dozen of the introverts I know.

The answer is that while extroverts may get some extra energy in their life by being in a cohort, introverts still benefit even though their approach to being in a cohort may be different. Whether we gain energy in crowds (extroverts) or drain energy in crowds (introvert), we all need the sense of identity, comradery and purpose that comes with being part of something we're not in control of.

Collaborators

Collaborators (literally, co-laborers) may be brought together by a third party or we may form our own group of collaborators. Either way, the purpose of the group of collaborators is the accomplishment of a task based upon the effort and contribution from each individual. If you conclude that collaborators are simply a cohort with a job to do, you wouldn't be entirely wrong but that "job to do" makes a huge amount of difference.

Let's go back to the classroom. In my previous example of my cohort mates, we were pursuing someone else's purpose — getting educated. We weren't determining the how, when, what, or why. We were simply showing up and learning individually, in parallel, even in a group setting.

Now fast forward a few years to college, and my first experience with what was, for me, a landmark group project.

I attended a small liberal arts college in the Chicago area, where interdisciplinary learning experiences were highly valued by the faculty and regularly dreaded by the students. One of those opportunities was a course that was required for everyone, no matter what their major, called "The Social Contract." Since the course was required, it was one of the largest classes in this small college which bragged about its class size and 1-to-6 faculty-to-student ratio.

This class was taught by five co-laboring professors — one from the arts, one from communications, one from science, one from the psychology/sociology department, and one from the philosophy/theology team.

The pinnacle assignment in this class was a group research paper: One paper to be produced by 6 people, and every individual in the group would receive the same grade. The grade would be based entirely on the finished product, and the project grade would be one third of the total class grade.

I was in a panic. The group was chosen for me, the topic of our paper would be chosen by the group, and my grade point average hung in the balance at the hands of other people.

I bet you've been in that situation — your grade, your raise, your job, or your success — depends upon other people doing their jobs well. Collaborators aren't necessarily our friends. They're not necessarily people we like, enjoy, or trust. They are, however, essential to the success of the task to which we've committed.

This was partly the point of the exercise. After all, the class was called "The Social Contract," and the focus was on the ways in which we do and do not work together in society.

Well, in my case, I didn't respond so well to the collaboration challenge. The short story is that through manipulation of everyone in the group, I ended up researching and writing at least 80% of the entire project and re-writing the other 20%. My solution was to convert a collaborative effort into a one-man show.

Although my grade (and everyone else's) was a shiny "A," that experience didn't fill me with a sense of accomplishment. Instead, it haunted me for years. Tragically, I had missed out on all the benefits of co-laboring: character, inclusion, and self-leadership.

"Iron sharpens iron" is an ancient phrase and one that my mother often repeated when I complained about people I didn't like working with (primarily my sisters.) As all wise mothers do, Mom often boiled down her wisdom into pithy sayings and quotations from authoritative sources — in this case, the wisdom of Solomon in Proverbs 27 (of the Judaic and Christian holy texts).

In fact, in ancient metallurgy, iron was hardened by heating it in charcoal (carbon) and hammering it with another piece of iron. The result was that the sword or implement being made became hard — and when it was used and worn, it could be refreshed in a similar manner: heating, beating, and bathing.

Just like iron, character has a chance to harden and to be refurbished amid co-laboring. As we work with others, we each have input into the process, and output from our efforts. We have expectations about how much each other will work, the quality of not only the outcome of the labor but of the effort going into the labor. We have differing opinions about how the labor should progress. All those expectations give opportunity for disappointment, and disappointment gives opportunity to anger, and anger gives opportunity for a choice — and choice is the birthplace of character.

In my college project, I bypassed as much of that co-laboring as I could and relied on charisma and talent to achieve my goals. As John Maxwell says, "Talent is a gift, but character is a choice. It's true that charisma can make a person stand out for a moment, but character sets a person apart for a lifetime."

A key value of co-laboring, especially in retirement, is to continue to build, sharpen and re-harden character. Just as the blacksmiths of old could revitalize a sword by re-heating it, pounding it, and plunging it into cold water, co-laboring keeps our character sharp and ready to withstand the trials of the second half of life.

Cohorts give us a valuable gift by lumping us together with diverse people and co-laboring deepens that gift by requiring us to yield, learn, and be led by divergent people. It could be that this aspect of co-laboring is exactly the part of being employed or running a business that you liked the least: putting up with other people who want to get

146

the job done in a different way. Perhaps this is one of the things you've been looking forward to in retirement: Doing things your own way.

I get that. I love doing things my way!

As I mentioned earlier, though, one of the biggest risks of retirement is the possibility of a homogenous life, in which everything and everyone is familiar, acceptable, and the same as us.

When we co-labored with others to produce income to pay down our debts and put food on the table, our stakes were higher. Now, to the extent that our co-laboring isn't totally about income, we can focus on the non-income rewards of co-laboring, including learning to learn from others with different ideas, backgrounds, values, and beliefs.

When we co-labor and include diverse people in our labor, we give opportunity to develop our self-leadership — observing our reactions and choosing our responses. The beauty of this phase of life is that our co-laboring can often be detached from our source of income, which makes it easier for us to be mindful and intentional in reaping the benefits of collaboration.

Co-creators

Co-creation is that intimate, self-yielding, other-centric act that brings intense pleasure to the co-creators, and results in something that lives, grows, and gains significance interdependently and independently from the creators. Sounds like sex and making babies, doesn't it?

Co-creation is more than making babies together, although that image is one that I want you to hold because it is the most readily understandable experience of co-creation we have in our lives.

When we are in a cohort, we come together because someone else has called us to come together. We gain identity with the group, but the cohort may not last once circumstances change. Cohorts can become co-laborers if they take ownership of the common purpose for which they are together.

In co-laboring, value is created by the whole for the individuals — we each put in our effort, we do the job together, and we take home a paycheck individually. There is a point at which co-laboring can become co-creation, and making babies is exactly the right image.

In cohorts, each person takes on the identity of the group, but serves their own purpose for being in the group and whatever reward they gain is primarily for them alone.

In collaborations, each person takes on the identity of the group, but serves the group purpose so each person can individually receive a reward.

In co-creation, each person chooses to contribute part of themselves to generate something that is beyond the sum of the contributions, bigger and separate from each of the co-creators, and the reward is for others first and for the creators second. Just like making a baby! Or just like Orville and Wilbur Wright's flying machine. Or just like Rogers and Hammerstein's musicals. Or just like Lennon and McCartney's songs.

I see that hand! "Can't I just create? Must I *co-create*?" Here are three ways that co-creation is superior to solo-creation:

Intention: When we co-create, we are, from the very start, yielding our self-interest to the interest of others. Our creativity is not generated from our ego-system, but instead within an eco-system. We add value to others during creation. As a result, our creation is more likely to add value to others.

Integration: When we co-create, we're in a place of integration, not insulation. Napoleon Hill, in the early 1900s, wrote about this integration when he spoke of the formation of a Master Mind when two or more come together in the co-creative process. This Master Mind has greater power and potential than the sum of the individuals.

Imperfection: When we solo-create, we're often certain that not only is the way we've created "right," but also the result. After all, we did what we did because it was the right thing, otherwise we wouldn't have done it! When we co-create, because we're continually yielding, compromising, and accepting, we know inherently that our creation is flawed.

Those "flaws" make our creation accessible to others. They bring value to others in ways we can't anticipate. Those flaws in our creation allow us to invite others to join in and contribute and improve, which in turn creates an ongoing legacy. Co-creation is generative in a way that solo-creation can never be.

Now Is The Time

Why is co-creation important in the second half of life? Primarily because most of us have not yet co-created (aside from making babies) in the first half.

Chances are, like most people, you have set aside your deepest desires, dreams and ambitions to pay the rent, buy the food, pay the tuition, keep the car running, raise the kids and get them married, and take a few vacations in the middle of all that.

Most likely, there is still something you want to accomplish, to create, to plant so it goes and grows beyond you and beyond your lifetime. (A great tool for helping you discover, define and pursue your dream is The Dream Test, which you can download free at http://bit.ly/MatesDream2) For those of us with children, we often point to them and declare "that's my legacy." That's true and good and worthwhile. Is it enough?

I have four marvelous children, scattered around the globe, each one of them serving the world in which they live in self-sacrificing ways. I'm rightfully proud of them and what they are doing and who they are, and yet they cannot be the sum of my life's purpose.

If my grandparents' destiny was to create and raise children, and my parents' destiny was to create and raise children, and my destiny is to create and raise children — well, you get the picture.

If leaving a legacy is just raising great kids, then soon raising great kids is all there is in life, and we're kicking the can down the road of history saying that the real significance of life is perpetually in the future. We totally negate the significance that can be found here and now.

Total transparency here: I'm a person of faith. I'm not interested in making you believe what I believe, but you should know that my ideas about co-creation are shaped by my belief that we've been created by a Creator. We've been created to create. We've been created for relationship. We've been created for significance.

Rusty Rustenbach, in *Giving Yourself Away* writes, "You and I live in an age when only a rare minority of individuals desire to spend their lives in pursuit of objectives which are bigger than they are. In our age, for most people, when they die it will be as though they never lived."

Again, quoting John Maxell: "Success can last a lifetime; significance can last several lifetimes."

You Need Them All

Here's your challenge: As you design the second half of your life — as you re-discover and define your passion and your purpose — gather your mates for the journey. Cohorts, collaborators, co-creators — you need all of them. You need the group identity of cohorts, you need the challenge and sharpening effect of co-laborers, and you need the intimacy and significance of co-creating. As many have said, the two greatest days of your life are the day you were born and the day you find out why. The third great day: When you die knowing that you've co-created something that is beyond yourself.

Cohort with others. Find collaborators. Co-create. Live the second half of life with purpose and significance. Find your mates.

About The Author

An Illinois native, Joel Shuflin now cohorts, collaborates and co-creates in Arizona. As an Executive Director with The John Maxwell Team, Joel has been mentored by John C. Maxwell and John's team in The Maxwell Method of Coaching. Joel coaches internationally with individuals and organizations in transition, including those individuals transitioning to retirement, stepping out of active business ownership, and seeking to build a legacy of significance. Joel can be reached by phone at 480-525-7240, or by visiting his website, joelshuflin.com. To download the Dream Test mentioned in this chapter, visit http://bit.ly/MatesDream2

Notes

1. Holt-Lunstad, Julianne, Timothy B. Smith, and J. Bradley Layton. "Social Relationships and

Mortality Risk: A Meta-analytic Review." *PLOS Medicine*, July 27, 2010. doi: https://doi.org/10.1371/journal.pmed.1000316.

2. Mlodinow, Leonard, *Subliminal: How Your Unconscious Mind Rules Your Behavior* (New York: Random House, 2012).

Go Be A Blessing in Your Season of Retirement

By Dale Chanaiwa

When I learned that RCA was publishing a book and looking for authors to contribute by writing a chapter, I was so excited. I thought "What a wonderful opportunity for us all to share the depth and breadth or our knowledge, expertise, education and life experiences in a way that can shape, make, or break your Season of Retirement. I'm all in!" Or so I thought.

As usual, it was not long before my self-doubt and fears, procrastination, and perfectionism kicked in.

Some of the doubts and fears that went through my head were: I have not achieved as much as the other authors, nor have I been coaching, as long; I am not a great writer or as good as everyone else; I have nothing to share that anyone would be interested in reading.

Once I decided I have something to contribute, procrastination set in. I will work on it later. I know the deadline, and I have plenty of time. I have too much going on in my life right now that requires my attention. And there was a lot of busyness going on in my life. Most of my busyness was being driven by others, work, family, and friends, which made it easy for me to continue to put off working on my chapter.

As if procrastination was not enough, perfectionism kicked in. Anytime I started to write I was never happy with the results. After all, as many as

154

hundreds, if not thousands of people will be reading this book. I must bring my best, but will it be good enough?

So, what got me unstuck and moving forward? Reflecting on one of my Diamond Dale Discoveries. My Diamond Dale Discoveries are what I call my "aha" moments. The Diamond Dale Discovery that put me back on track is "Today is not just another day and another dollar. Today is another opportunity to be a blessing in someone's life, and that is priceless." Let me share with you how I made this discovery.

While employed by a healthcare maintenance organization, I had the privilege to know and work with "a certain woman" who was a customer services representative in the call center. She passed away under the age of 55. I am sure she never imagined she would pass away at such a young age. Indeed, none of her co-workers did.

She loved what she did each day. She was a staunch advocate for our Medicare members. She was always, willing, ready and able to assist members with a compassionate heart. Members would call for assistance and ask for her specifically. Often, they were willing to wait, if necessary, to speak to her, only.

She never reached retirement age. But, she lived each day as if it was another opportunity to be a blessing in someone's life. You can't put a price on being a blessing in someone's life. Whether you are

155

nearing retirement, entering retirement or have transitioned to retirement, you must remember, whether good or bad, your actions and words impact the lives of others. A smile, a word of encouragement or lack thereof, can be the turning point in someone's life.

Tomorrow is not promised. No matter what you envision doing in your Season of Retirement, be sure you have an answer for: What am I doing today to make a difference in the lives of others? What am I doing today to bring someone joy? As you continue your journey, whatever, you decide the best way to utilize your time, talents and treasures, will be, always remember, "Today is not just another day and another dollar. Today is another opportunity to be a blessing in someone's life, and that is priceless."

Go Be A Blessing in Your Season of Retirement!

About The Author

Known as an encourager and facilitator, Dr. Dale Chanaiwa is a motivational speaker, life coach, retirement coach, mentor, and published author. She has a doctorate degree in law and more than 40 years of knowledge and expertise in the healthcare and business development industries. She has created multiple programs designed to empower women to enhance their added-value. Your added-value is comprised of your gifts, talents, expertise, education, and life experiences that make you a unique individual, destined to do what you have been called to do. For additional information regarding programs and services offered, please visit her website, www.seasonedsassysisterhood.com, or email her at seasonedsassysister@gmail.com.

Living A Sensory-Driven Life

By Brenda M. Carrico

What motivates you? For me, it is death. Yes, as strange as that may sound to you, it's death. I come from a large family and I've always had lots of friends and with that comes large loss.

I've attended funerals since I was able to walk and talk. I've witnessed how short or how long life can be. Death does not discriminate — taking the ones I love from between the ages of 4 to 96 years old.

So, this is why death motivates me and why I often think about my own inevitable final day. It's why I do my best to live in the moment. To treat the people I love, when I'm with them, as though it may be the last time we see each other.

Living in the moment doesn't just apply to exciting or profound experiences. It applies to everything we do, including going through the motions of our daily routines.

I often find myself watching my husband from across the room. Paying attention to his every movement — the subtle expressions on his face, the way he walks and talks. It's an intentional practice, so if I find myself living this life without him one day these memories are forever imprinted in my mind.

Since I've lost so many friends and family over the years, I know every day is a gift and everyday could be my last. Because I know that I have to financially plan as though I may live a long life, I choose to live a little along the way and make sure I save some money to spend later. What I'm saving to spend another day is intended for me to have a fulfilling retirement, if I'm lucky enough to make it there. Yes, there are many of us who won't make it to retirement age.

The final chapters of life will look different for everyone. Some of you may never want to retire. You love your job and going to work every day brings you a sense of purpose and fulfillment. Others may never be able to afford it for various reasons. Some of us are thrown into it via forced retirement, disability or having to take care of a family member. Whatever the case, make sure you take time to do the things that bring you pleasure.

Whether you retire or continue working until the day you die, you should always do your best to live as though each minute could be the one where you draw your final breath. As the Tim McGraw song goes, "Live like you were dying."

Start being purposeful when designing your life and make sure it isn't all about the paycheck, working 24/7. What's the point in working if you can't take some of those hard-earned dollars to have a little fun? Begin by allocating a few hours on the weekend to do the things you enjoy.

Did you forget what that is? Well let's reawaken your inquisitive side. To get started, think about what you would do if you lost any of your five senses — sight, smell, hearing, taste and touch, or possibly your seventh sense. I say seventh because, typically, intuition is referred to as your sixth. For our purposes, the seventh sense is your mind or your memory.

Grab a journal or notepad to jot down your thoughts. Dedicate at least one page to each of your senses because I guarantee once you get started and your mind starts spinning, you're going to come up with a plethora of ideas and you'll wish you had additional space to write.

Eyesight

One day at work, I was reading a training manual. I became really frustrated and complained to my coworkers about the poor quality of print. "How do they expect people to learn this if they can't even read it?" I asked a coworker if I could borrow their reading glasses to see if magnifying it (wink, wink) would help. Voilà! I could suddenly see the material. I realized I needed reading glasses. Oh well! I sure wasn't going to give up my love of reading.

What if one day your eye doctor informed you that you have macular degeneration or some other condition that will affect your vision as you age? What are the things you would want to see for the first time, or one more time before something like this happened — The Green Monster, Grand Canyon, Eiffel Tower, snowcapped mountains, flipping through the pages of old photo albums? Most definitely (for me) the faces of the ones I love.

Hearing

You suddenly realize you have to keep turning the television up louder and louder to hear your favorite show. At first you think something is wrong with the program you're watching. Then you think it's your television set. The sound must be going out on it. Finally, you conclude that the real problem is you are losing your hearing.

If this is an easy fix by getting a hearing aid, do it! Don't be stubborn because you don't want to admit your body is changing and you don't want to be embarrassed that you need this device to hear.

I ask you, how is this any different than getting eye glasses? They are visual aids. So, why miss out on the thrill of hearing an Indy car zoom by, the relaxing sound of a pod of orcas blowing as they glide through the sea, a baby's laugh, a thunderstorm, your favorite song, or your partner's voice, if you don't have to.

Just like smells, hearing can help us recall special memories as well. Whenever I hear the song, "In the Mood" by the Glenn Miller Band, I can visualize my parents swing dancing. What do you want to be able to hear?

Taste

You go in for your annual check-up and after the results of your blood work come back your physician says you must cut back on your sodium intake. This sounds simple enough, until you start paying attention to how much sodium is in everything you eat.

For some, eating isn't just about the multisensory experience. In our society, many of our social events are planned around sharing a meal with family and friends. Even if food no longer tastes the same, make sure you still permit yourself to appreciate the company.

Not every meal is going to be the best thing you ever ate. But you surely have, what I like to call, my "death-row meals." The things you would want to eat one last time.

That said, if something happened and your favorite foods and beverages no longer tasted the same, what would you want to savor one more time: a greasy cheeseburger, a New-York-style pizza (in New York), chicken tikka masala (in India), a medium-rare steak with a loaded baked potato, or your favorite beverage?

If you like trying new culinary delights, what are those you've always wanted to try but haven't yet? Do you want to go to a celebrity chef restaurant and try their food?

Touch

Hugs! My family is a hugging family. You don't dare say good-bye and think you're going to walk out the door without giving out hugs.

My father passed away over five years ago. He was sick for a while, so when I accepted the fact that he wouldn't be with us much longer those hugs became longer and tighter. To this day, the memories of those hugs still get me through the tough times.

If you knew you would develop a condition like peripheral neuropathy and lose your sense of touch, what would you want to feel before this happened? Would it be a warm shower, soft sheets, petting a horse's mane, swimming with a dolphin, going to one of those spas where the fish nibble on your feet, or your partner caressing your face or rubbing your back?

Smell

If you've ever driven down a country road, you might smell things that you find pungent and make you want to pinch your nose. For me, those same smells evoke fond memories, reminding me of visits to my aunt and uncle's farm. For over 50 years, my family has celebrated the Fourth of July there. When I was young, they would take us on hayrides. We would sleep out under the stars on their wagons.

We've all had experiences of smelling something that seems familiar and it transports us back to another place and time. The smell of roses reminds me of my Aunt Mary and Uncle Joe's house. Fresh baked pies and bread remind me of walking through the front door of my grandparents' house.

Normal aging alone can cause us to lose our sense of smell. If you knew you were about to lose yours what do you want to smell again so the memory is so strong you can still recall what something smells like even if you can't actually smell it. Or, what is something you've never smelled and want to — salty sea air, walking through a chocolate factory, rain falling, flowers, food, your favorite perfume, or a musty old book?

To give you some additional ideas, see "Holiday Ideas For Your Five Senses: Food, Sounds, Smells, Sights And Touch".[1]

The Mind

Many years ago, I attended a Rotary meeting and the guest speaker's topic was Alzheimer's disease. She said something that really stuck with me through the years — some patients, not all, but some who were diagnosed with the disease were able to improve their memory once they started brain training.

There are a multitude of studies that indicate we may be able to prevent or minimize memory loss due to aging if we perform mentally stimulating activities. You will also find articles stating that using all your senses can improve learning and brain function.

There are a few, like the one referenced below, that state the reverse is true as well. Learning something new can sharpen your senses. We all know there are benefits to keeping our minds active, it's just a matter of whether we actually do so.

In an article published at *Be Brain Fit*, the author states, "brain exercise is reported to help in all these areas: less stress, better memory, more positive mood, increased focus and concentration, boost in motivation and productivity, enhanced fluid intelligence, creativity, and mental flexibility, faster thinking and reaction time, greater self-confidence, sharper vision and hearing."[2]

Do some research and find a brain training program such as BrainHQ or Lumosity that works best for you. If you don't have a computer, buy a crossword puzzle or a Sudoku book. Go to the library and check out a book on a subject that you don't know anything about. Learn a new language. Whatever you decide, do something to keep your mind active.

Alzheimer's is not the only threat to memory loss. You could be in an accident, have a stroke, or have any number of things happen that could forever alter your ability to function in the same way.

Unless something like this happens to you, remember, getting older doesn't mean you have to get old. You can do things to stave off the aging process. Do your best to stay healthy and vibrant by eating right, exercising and performing activities that stimulate your mind. If you're not doing these things now, you should start so they become habits.

Putting Your Senses To Use

The odds are that your senses have already been driving how you live your life; what you eat, where you travel and the fragrances you buy for example.

At this stage of your life, though, it's probably on autopilot and you've taken it for granted.

It's time to be purposeful about living a sensory-driven life — partially to keep them fine-tuned and partially to create memories of what something looks, tastes or smells like in the unfortunate event that one or more of your senses deteriorates or you lose them altogether. Make sure you are enjoying life by putting your senses to use while you still can.

Life is full of challenges, changes, and sadness. Balance these moments by participating in things that bring you happiness. If you are stumped about what that is, revive your sleeping inner child and stoke the flame of curiosity that long ago became a flicker because you got so busy at the business of life — that part of you that was asking why the sky is blue and the grass is green.

Begin by exploring the city you live in. I'm always amazed by the number of people who don't know about all the wonderful things there are available to do right in their own backyard.

We were traveling with a tour group once and some of our fellow travelers included a family that lived just outside of Philadelphia. For a history buff like me, living anywhere in the Northeast would make me feel like a kid in a candy store. Yet, this family had never even taken their children to see the Liberty Bell or Independence Hall. How do you live so close to the place where the United States Constitution was drafted and not visit?

Well, retirement — as is your entire life — is a unique experience. Just because this would be important to me does not mean it would be important to you. So, what is important to you?

You have the freedom to write the script for every minute of your day. This may be intimidating at first, but once you start asking yourself what you would like to know more about, places you would like to visit, or hobbies you want to try, I will bet you'll be surprised at what long-forgotten desires and wishes start to resurface or how many things interest you that you are just beginning to realize.

Even though the term "bucket list" has gotten a bad rap of late, I still encourage you to make one. I have a bucket list. As I'm reading articles, I write down what intrigues me and I'm constantly adding to it. Whether you're retired yet or not, start keeping track of all the things you want to do or learn.

In addition to the list I keep on my desk, I have a folder in my email titled "retirement articles." I email myself articles about things I want to see and do, road trips I want to take in the U.S., or different places I would like to live for three to six months at a time, so I can become fully immersed in different cultures, which is great for the brain by the way.

In an article published by the *Huffington Post*, "10 Proven Ways To Grow Your Brain: Neurogenesis And Neuroplasticity," travel is named as one of these ways. "Those new and challenging situations cause the brain to sprout dendrites. (A short branched extension of a nerve cell.) You don't need to travel across the world to reap these benefits either; taking a weekend road trip to a different city gives your brain the same stimulation."[3]

House Hunters International, a television show on HGTV, is research for me. I discover places I want to visit and potentially live for a short stint someday. I don't want to just live vicariously through these episodes and other people's lives. I want to be that person staying overseas, tasting new foods, seeing historical sites in Europe or Asia. This would be a dream come true for me. What would be a dream come true for you?

Start planning your life as though it is your job. Retirement offers the gift of time to do the things that matter most to you. Knowing what that is prior to transitioning into this next stage of life should help ease the uncertainty that surrounds the decision to stop working.

You planned for college or a job immediately following high school. You planned for your family. You planned financially for retirement. Now, it's time to plan your fun so you don't sit on the couch wondering, "What did I just do?" or, "What do I do now?"

Retiring from a paid job doesn't mean retiring from life. Use one or more of your senses by relaxing, reading, writing, studying, singing, dancing, researching your family tree, throwing pottery, joining an astronomy club, becoming a political activist, learning a new language, learning how to play the piano, or going to the movies, the opera, or a Broadway production. You've imagined what this moment would be like and now you're finally here. Live it to the fullest.

Remember, you don't have to be extremely wealthy to have fun. If you're on a fixed income, you can still enjoy this phase of life. Search your community for free or inexpensive activities. I've done this when living on a tight budget, so I know these opportunities exist.

You can be a ticket taker at the performing arts theater and maybe get to see the shows for free. Go to the library and check out a book or movie. The city where I live, as well as some of the neighboring towns, have free outdoor concerts in the spring and summertime. The local arboretum has days of the week that are free to visitors.

Every town has parks and picnic areas where you can just go to soak up (feel) the warm sun, smell the wild flowers, and share a meal together (taste). The main art museum in my city is free — you just have to pay for parking. Don't forget to take advantage of senior discounts.

Since you are also supposed to be enjoying life before retirement (in case you don't make it to retirement age), if you have a fear of running out of money, then make sure you do the big-ticket items on your bucket list before you step away from your job, knowing you can replenish the coffer.

Retiring also doesn't mean you're no longer going to be a contributing member of society. Allocate time for some charitable/philanthropic endeavors. You can now go to communities that have just been impacted by a natural disaster to help at a moment's notice. Help with literacy programs, volunteer at a pet shelter — whatever touches your heart and feeds your soul.

Once you've created your list, prioritize what you want to do the most and front load your retirement with those activities. If you are married, you will want to select the adventures you want to experience together should one of you pass earlier than the other. I'm sure every one of you has had a friend that dreamed about spending their golden years with their partner, but they were short-lived or never came. If you're the surviving partner, don't throw out your bucket list. The remaining items will help keep you going once your other half is gone.

As you know, the older we get, the more we have to permanently say good-bye to the people we love. So just like you scheduled appointments at work, schedule appointments to visit your friends and family. My guess is there are a lot of people who would be thrilled to hear from you. Please don't get stuck in the, "Well the phone rings both ways" loop.

It is true, retirement is no doubt a luxury and for many it is a foreign concept. But if retirement is a possibility for you and it's what you want, and you feel comfortable with the amount you've saved, then take the leap when you're ready.

Retirement is about finally having the balance part of the work-life balance we're all striving for. Let's face it — for many, the balance during their working years is non-existent, especially if you're raising children. So, the balance comes when you finally get to retire from your paying job.

This is the period of your life when you're no longer coming home after a 10- to 12-hour workday feeling brain dead and physically exhausted. Nor do you have to worry about being a "responsible" adult, to a degree.

You actually have the energy to do something other than go to work, clean your house or do yardwork. You can quit setting your alarm clock, unless of course you need to get up for an early flight or hit the road for your next adventure.

My parents traveled wherever they wanted and designed a life for themselves surrounded by the most amazing group of friends anyone could ever ask for. They are the poster group for living, laughing, learning and loving together — the perfect retirement. Thank God they have such a wonderful network of friends because they were a Godsend for my mother when my father passed away.

Retirement will look different for everyone and the age at which you do it is a personal choice. Know that your time will now be your own! What are you going to do with it? What would you regret not doing before you draw your final breath?

For those of you who say you're afraid to retire because you're worried you'll be bored or run out of things to do, tap into your senses and the answers will come to you.

About The Author

Throughout her time in the financial planning industry, Brenda Carrico, APMA®, CPRC, FQPQ™, has met countless people who express their worries and fears about retirement. She uses her training as a Certified Professional Retirement Coach to help people find joy and purpose in every stage of life. She also equips individuals with tools to discuss retirement and aging with their friends and loved ones, so each person can feel fully supported during their transition to retirement. Brenda is a Financial Paraplanner Qualified Professional™ and an Accredited Portfolio Management Advisor[SM]. Connect with Brenda at www.linkedin.com/in/brendacarrico.

Notes

1. Brian Johnston, "The World's Best Places for Sight, Sound, Smell, Taste and Touch," *Traveller*, March 15, 2017, http://www.traveller.com.au/travel-for-the-senses-guyc9w.

2. Deane Alban, "15 Brain Exercises to Keep Your Mind Sharp," *Be Brain Fit*, June 17, 2018, https://bebrainfit.com/brain-exercises/.

3. Thai Nguyen, "10 Proven Ways To Grow Your Brain: Neurogenesis And Neuroplasticity," *The Huffington Post*, December 07, 2017, https://www.huffingtonpost.com/thai-nguyen/10-proven-ways-to-grow-yo_b_10374730.html.

Life For Me Without You: Preparing and Coping

By Brenda M. Carrico

Whether you are younger or older, newly married or married for a while, losing a partner is always difficult; especially after 20-plus years. It may feel like you've lost your dominant arm and you have to acclimate and figure out how to function all over again.

It can seem overwhelming and you may ask yourself how you are ever going to get through it. I imagine this is even more difficult for those who have never lived alone. They went from living with their parents to living with their partner.

While you will never be able to fully prepare for the emotions and the dramatic transition that will occur in your life after your partner is gone, there are many things you can do that will act as a guiding light in the middle of the chaos.

Some are habits and processes that we should technically start as soon as we move in together. However, we often start performing what were once considered traditional roles or roles that come easier to one or the other as soon as we step into our new home together.

One of you feels more comfortable doing the cooking and cleaning while the other seems better suited for handling the household finances while also taking care of yardwork and general home maintenance.

You would think after decades of both men and women being in the workforce that many of our domestic chores would be things that we do together as a team. But I still see young couples repeating these traditions; right or wrong.

Maybe you're intimidated by managing the household finances or certain home maintenance projects because you think it's more complicated than it actually is. But if something happens to the partner who handles these things, disability or death, you need to be able to pick up and keep going with the practical side of life without skipping a beat.

When we're younger, if something were to happen to the partner who handled certain tasks, it's easier to adapt. We haven't relied on them and grown accustomed to them taking care of their duties for 40-plus years.

However, if you've fallen into the habit of letting your partner handle something for decades and you, unexpectedly or expectedly, have to start taking care of everything, it may feel like you're learning how to tie your shoes again.

As long as you are both still breathing and able, it's never too late to start treating certain components of your marriage like a job — a partnership if you will.

There is always someone, at least at most companies, who knows how to do your job so that things can still be taken care of while you are on vacation or if you suddenly decided to quit (retire). Cross-training your partner is one of the greatest gifts you can give them. Being a grateful recipient of that gift is just as important.

Much like a business owner should do, create a succession plan for your family.

Practical

One of you is the quintessential handyperson — you can repair anything. What is your partner going to do when you are no longer there to fix the leaky faucet or the backed-up drain? Do they know how to change the air filter on the furnace, what size to buy, and the frequency with which it needs to be done? What about the alarm on the sump pump? Do they know how to shut it off or do they have to sit and listen to an annoying beep while they fumble around trying to figure it out.

Some of these things you can put off dealing with until they reach a point of irritation or it persists and gets worse (for example, when the leaky faucet becomes a steady stream of water).

Maybe you have children who could fix it, but you don't want to bother them, or they live in a different state. Possibly you've moved into a maintenance-free community at this point, but they don't typically deal with interior maintenance.

Similar to finding a life mate, you're going to have to kiss a lot of toads before you find a "handyprince(ss)" that you feel comfortable having in your home. So that you know you're leaving your partner in good hands, consider hiring contractors before one of you is gone so you can both decide if they're dependable.

There are certain meals that your partner cooks that are your favorites. When they're in the kitchen cooking, you're sitting in the living room watching television taking in the smells wafting through the air. Your mouth is watering as you sit in your recliner waiting for them to tell you dinner is ready.

Do they have the recipe filed away somewhere? Even if they did, would you know where to find it or how to cook it? It's time to get out of the living room and into the kitchen. Have your partner teach you not only how to make the meal but where to find all the ingredients.

Not only will you be creating new memories together, you'll be able to cook the dish for yourself if they pass away before you. Even if you don't ever make it after they're gone, you're learning a life skill that will keep you from eating all your meals at restaurants — unless that's what you want to do, and you can afford it.

Other, everyday practical things we just do and forget the one we love the most in the world may not know how to do, include:

- Use the remote control(s)

- Rebooting the cable box

- Logging into the computer and all of the electronic accounts that you have individually or together

- How to use the DVR

- Adjusting the settings on the humidifier when the seasons change

- Changing air and water filters

- How to shut off the main water line

- Using the washer and dryer

- Car maintenance

- Lawn maintenance/snow removal

The list goes on and on. Spend time walking through your house, making an inventory of these things and writing down instructions.

Identify your preferred style of communication: hand written, typed and saved on your computer or in the cloud, or sent in an email.

It may be best if each of you write your own set of instructions, so it makes the most sense to you. Remember, one of you won't be there to ask questions if you don't understand what the other wrote.

Once you've decided which works for both of you, decide on a filing system that will make it easy for each of you to locate the instructions you're looking for.

I don't know if my dad did it for his benefit or my mother's but, after he passed away, she started finding notes taped on certain appliances around the house with instructions on how to do something.

This alone will not help you think of everything so each time you are performing general maintenance, cutting the grass, taking the car for an oil change, cooking, doing the laundry, or something as simple as dusting and knowing where to find the polish and dust cloth, ask your partner if they know where, what, and how. If not, add it to your instructions or start sharing these tasks.

You may be sitting there thinking my partner has common sense. They should be able to figure it out after I'm gone. Or, you tell yourself if they look, they'll eventually be able to find what they're searching for. Under normal circumstances, they probably could.

This is one of the problems with falling into the habit of traditional role assignments. One of you has just died after 40-plus years of marriage — this is not under normal circumstances. Something as simple as trying to find a skillet, and not being able to, can send a person over the edge.

Your partner is lost, confused, and trying to make their way through a dark room with nothing more than a match to light their way. Teaching your partner these routine things before you're gone gives them a flood light instead.

Financial

This is a topic that countless books have been written about and one that cannot be covered in a section of a single chapter so think of this as just a starting point.

Many of us are intimated by basic finances. However, if you haven't already done it, it's time to put your financial house in order. As with anything in life, the more you educate yourself, the less intimidating it becomes. You may also find that once you understand it, you may feel empowered and more self-confident.

Let's start with some common items that can cause unintended consequences for your partner after one of you has passed:

You purchased your home and called the utility companies to turn on your utilities. When they asked you for contact information, you gave them your details, but you didn't think to provide them with your partner's.

This seems harmless enough, right? There wasn't any ill will when you did this. However, should something happen to you, the living partner who's not named on the account will still need service. Utility companies frequently charge a deposit if you have no history with them. Having both names on the bill avoids this issue. It also permits the partner who is not currently named to make changes to service or call for repairs.

My mother had a friend who contacted a utility company for a service call after her husband passed away. Not only did they refuse to come out and take care of the issue until her name was on the account, they threatened to turn off her utilities if she didn't provide them with the deposit immediately.

Maybe you have a partner who spends too much, so you didn't want them to have access to certain funds. Or, you're the partner who balances the checkbook and pays all the bills. In these scenarios, you decided to put all your savings and checking accounts in your name and didn't add your partner as a joint owner to any of them. These are also probably the accounts that your Social Security, pension and other retirement benefits are being deposited into.

You also didn't name your partner as a beneficiary on the accounts. Although, you may have had good intentions when you did this, you've left them penniless until they can hire an attorney and go through probate court.

On average, probate can take 6-9 months to complete. Other complications can cause this process to take longer. This means that it could be a year or more before your partner once again has access to your life savings and can financially care for themselves.

Yes, these are extreme scenarios and things would rarely play out this way. But I want to convey to you the importance of handling these issues so that the living partner hopefully doesn't have to deal with any variation of these circumstances after the passing of the other.

First on your agenda — add them to at least your primary checking account. Even if only as a Transfer on Death (TOD) beneficiary designation. Next, run, don't walk, to an estate planning attorney and either update or prepare your documents. Stop putting this off and telling yourself you have time to take care of it.

Whether you're 20 or 75 years old, you never know what kind of a hand life will deal you and how everything can change in an instant. So, take care of this before it's too late and your surviving partner is stuck doing reactionary planning.

It's not enough to just prepare the documents, you need to reregister accounts and update beneficiaries as instructed or it was a waste of your time and money.

This isn't just about taking care of the finances; you need to have a HealthCare Power of Attorney drawn up so that your partner or other trusted party can act as a medical advocate for you.

Maybe you think going to an estate planning attorney is too expensive, but did you know that if your partner has to go through probate court it may cost them even more — not just in time, but money.

"After adding up all of these fees and costs, you can count on probate taking anywhere from 3-8% of your assets away from your beneficiaries, which doesn't include estate and income taxes that may be due and payable during the course of the probate administration."[1]

As with the practical chores, if you have not already, create your first-aid kit for finances:

- Contact information for your healthcare insurance provider. Start walking your partner through the annual enrollment process for Medicare and any retiree health insurance benefits that you may still be eligible for.

- Contact information for your property casualty, home, and auto insurance providers

- Pension benefits

- Military benefits

- Utility company information (gas, water, cable, phone, etc.) including account and phone numbers. If an online account has been established, keep track of the usernames and passwords.

- Bank accounts; savings, checking, money market, certificates of deposit, etc.

- Brokerage accounts, including custodians and account numbers

- Financial advisors' contact information, if you're working with one

- Social Security benefits

- Tax preparer — if you're doing this yourself and your surviving partner would be absolutely lost, it may be time to find someone dependable to do this for them after you're gone.

- Digital assets (Shutterfly and iTunes accounts, for example)

- Credit cards

As with your household chores, this is just a sampling of what the surviving partner will need to know. Yes, at first it will be overwhelming, so take small steps. Don't spend a day drowning each other in data.

The next time you get an auto insurance invoice, go through it together. If you're out running errands, drop by your property casualty agent's office to introduce the partner who hasn't met them yet. If it is tax season, let the non-tax preparer know what documents they need to watch for in the mail to take to the accountant or prepare the returns themselves.

If you're working with a financial advisor, they may be able to assist you with organizing some, or all this information. If not, there are resources that are available to help you accomplish this.

If you prefer to do this online, consider Everplans.com or similar services. If you don't like technology, you can buy books that will guide you through this process. Not a Googler? Go to the library or a bookstore and look for resources.

If you have established relationships with any of the above referenced (property casualty agent, financial advisor, etc.), or if your non-financial partner has not already met these people or been included in meetings, it's time to start dragging them along — kicking and screaming, if necessary. It's for their own good.

Consider purchasing your burial plots in advance to ensure that your final resting places are next to each other. If you are uncertain where to start and what to consider, begin by visiting the following websites or actual funeral homes:

- https://beremembered.com

- http://funeralplan.com/funeralplan/preneed/index.html

- https://Parting.com

One or both of you will probably be resistant to some or all of this. Keep reminding yourselves that this is your parting gift to each other. You want to know that if anything happens, disability or death, the surviving partner will be okay if you're unable to help or you're deceased.

I've noticed as we get older, if there is something we don't know or understand, we're more frustrated by our ignorance than when we were younger. Maybe it's because now we are aware of our ignorance where we weren't as a child. We think as adults we should know everything. So, I encourage you to get over this feeling and, much like when you were a child, don't be afraid to ask for help.

You may go fast, or you may die after a prolonged illness, but when you're dying from a terminal illness the last thing you want to be worrying about is getting everything in order. Some days you can barely stay awake from taking pain meds. If the caretaker partner knows that all these things are already in place it's one less thing they have to worry about as your time on earth together draws to an end.

No one likes to think about death, let alone plan for it. However, by doing so, you relieve your family of having to make important financial decisions during a period of great stress and grief.

Legacy

Many people equate legacy planning to leaving their family a monetary inheritance. I encourage you to look at it from a different perspective.

I started genealogy research when I was a teenager. If I could have read letters and journals written by my ancestors it would have been an amazing experience for me. You don't have to be Shakespeare to write from your heart or just compose bullet points. For example, "I received free front row seats to Elton John." Enough said.

These are things that can be passed down from generation to generation. Not everyone is going to appreciate it, but someone will. In most cases, it will last a lot longer than your money.

Consider writing a legacy letter. This is a way to speak directly to your loved ones and say all those things you wish you had told them earlier. This letter can be a way to ensure your partner or children know how much joy your relationship brought, and you hope they will find happiness after you're gone.

If it is easier, enlist someone's help to record video for you. Ask friends and family to be a part of the video; imagine the people you love sitting around reminiscing with each other about all the special moments you've shared together. For those of you that are camera shy, this may distract you from the fact that you're being recorded.

Write your own eulogy. This process can help you discover more about yourself. It may also evoke strong emotions and seem challenging as you recall the journey that brought you to this place in your life. But it can be deeply beneficial.

For additional ideas about documenting your life for your children and future generations as well as organizing your financial life, I suggest you read the book, *Read This When I'm Dead* by Annie Presley and Christy Howard.

Emotional

It is impossible to prepare someone emotionally for the loss of a partner or loved one. Watching a family member suffer from a serious illness is taxing for everyone, but no one more so than the partner who is now playing the role of caretaker. They may find themselves being resentful of the sick partner for any number of reasons.

They feel trapped in the house and just want to get out for some fresh air. They want life to go back to the way it used to be. They want to continue doing all the things they did with their partner but now the sick partner doesn't feel up to it.

Give yourself permission to feel this way. Push the guilt you are experiencing aside. Missing what once was and wishing it would be a certain way again is part of the grieving process. You are coming to terms with the fact that your life is dramatically changing and you're about to start a new chapter without your partner by your side.

Preferably, before one of you is sick, have a health care plan. I'm not talking whether you're going to use BlueCross/BlueShield or Humana. I'm referring to having the uncomfortable discussion of when/if and for how long you want life-sustaining measures taken to keep you alive. What is the plan when the caretaking partner can no longer physically care for the sick partner, or when the need exceeds what the caretaker is capable of handling?

For the last two weeks of my dad's life, he just kept telling my mother, "Do not resuscitate! Do *not* resuscitate!" When the time came, it was already decided between the two of them. It doesn't make it any easier to let go, but it does make it easier for them to make the decision to take the medical measures necessary to let you go.

Whether people say it out loud or not, and they may not even realize it until their partner is gone, they were their best friend. Yes, they may have been referring to Joe or Mary as their best friends, but their partner was truly the one.

You didn't have to call them to see if they wanted to go to a movie or out to eat. They were always there. You ate together, ran errands together, traveled together, and played together. Now they're gone.

While they may have been your best friend, the circle of friendships you develop will be just as important during this stage of your life as any other. Whether you are an extrovert or an introvert, making and maintaining friendships to keep you from becoming a recluse should be a priority.

Should one of you become seriously ill, shifting the other into full-time caregiving, your true friends will understand that you are not neglecting the relationship and they will be there in any way they can. Keep their contact information handy so you can call to chat or invite them over for coffee for a well-needed mental-health break.

These friends will become a lifeline for the surviving partner. They will be the people who help you walk out your front door again and face the world without your other half. They will be the individuals who will keep you from falling into a deep depression.

I would recommend having friends from all age groups. Some of my best friends are, or have been, anywhere from 10 to 20 years older or younger than me. You get the wisdom from the friends who are older, and you can impart it to those who are younger. And, as awful as this may sound, you hopefully won't be the one who outlives all the others if you have a few that are younger.

If you've lost a partner, you understand that the air in your own home becomes thick with a silence that you didn't even know existed. Yes, you knew silence when you were in the same room together, but it was a comfortable silence. Even if you weren't saying anything to each other, there was a feeling of security by their mere presence.

This silence is different — it's a deafening silence. It's a stillness that causes you to hear white noise and ringing in your ears. The kind that makes you realize you're now alone. The type that makes you question your own sanity.

If you've never known this quiet before, or witnessed it, it will come. It appears when the crowds leave after the funeral services and your family goes home after spending that first week or two with you.

Unfortunately, it probably won't come slowly. It will come rushing at you like a raging bull or a massive swell. Be prepared to be knocked off your feet and have your breath taken away. Reach out to your friends when this happens. The good ones will be there to extend their hands to help you up again.

My parents, and now my mother, have a great network of friends. She has been calling one couple her "State Farm" neighbors because of the generosity and kindness they have shown her since my dad passed. The husband shovels the snow or helps her with lawnmower maintenance. Periodically, they'll invite her out to dinner. If you have a neighbor like this, treasure them and show them your gratitude because they are a rare find these days.

We can all only hope that we're lucky enough to have someone in our life to support us when we lose our own partner. No matter how many friends you have, in the quiet of the night, when the world has gone to sleep, your heart and your mind won't, and you will feel the pain of that loss all over again.

When you finally start to see clearly again, allow yourself to dream once more. Keep living, call on the network of friendships — that you developed before you lost your partner — to travel, share meals, go to the movies, or do anything that you share in common.

Not everyone has to be your confidant. You can reserve that status for a select few but you can have many friends that you do certain things with; going to the opera or an art museum. If there are things in which someone can't join you, then go alone.

With time, you may find that you prefer this on occasion. You can go see whatever movie you want at whatever time. You can go see an exhibit at a museum that interests you and spend as much time as you like without worrying about whether your friend is ready to leave before you.

When someone first passes away, the survivor is constantly being told to wait a year before they make any major decisions. Since we continuously hear this statement, as a society, I think we've conditioned ourselves to believe the survivor is suddenly okay after one year.

Things don't miraculously get better at that one-year mark. The surviving partner will have a void in their heart that will last until the day they die. Yes, life goes on and the pain subsides, but the ache, the sadness, and the occasional bout of loneliness creeps in like a stranger in the night.

To the children of the surviving parent, I implore you to spend quality time with them. If you live close by, visit them at least every other week. Don't do it for the first year and then stop — 26 days out of 365 is not that much in the whole scheme of things.

You have to eat at some point. Invite them to share a meal with you. If you understand how lonely meals can be for them, then you will be able to grasp the magnitude that this one gesture alone holds. Think about it — they're eating by themselves for the first time in decades.

If you don't live nearby, a weekly phone call will be more appreciated than you can even imagine. Set aside some of your vacation time to visit them. Remember, none of us is going to be here forever.

The sentimental days — wedding anniversaries, birthdays — the date of death will continue to be difficult. At the very least, reach out to the survivor on these days to check in on them. If you can, do something with them to get them out of the house because these milestones will always be tough to get through. Let them decide if they want to celebrate anniversaries and birthdays or they merely want to occupy their time for the day so they have something else to think about.

Just know one day this same loneliness will find its way into your life. When it does, you're going to understand how important it is to be there for your loved ones well beyond the first year after a partner passes.

As the survivor, you need to communicate to your children and your friends what you need. Let's face it, sometimes people just aren't hard wired to pick up on other's emotions.

Just like after your first few years of living together, when you realized things would go much smoother if you quit expecting your partner to read your mind, the same goes with your family and friends. Verbalize your needs. You will be disappointed less frequently and some of your sadness will be alleviated.

When a lifelong partner dies, you're going to feel like you're living in a fog for some time. Therefore, it is important to have your first aid kit — the kit that is going to assist you in continuing to manage the home alone and start doing all the chores that you once shared with your partner.

Part of this includes maintaining friendships, even during the times when you don't feel like getting out of bed and opening the curtains to let in the sun. Pull out your bucket list and continue to check things off it. You have to keep living.

If your partner gave you a present that you've always wanted, you wouldn't turn it down. So, if they try to cross-train you in the tasks that they take care of around the house or provide you guidance for making end-of-life decisions for them, don't refuse — it's a gift of genuine love.

They want to make sure that you will be taken care of when they're gone. No matter what your love language is, you can surely understand that your partner is trying to give you a gift that will continue to provide as long as you are still alive.

About The Author

Throughout her time in the financial planning industry, Brenda Carrico, APMA®, CPRC, FQPQ™, has met countless people who express their worries and fears about retirement. She uses her training as a Certified Professional Retirement Coach to help people find joy and purpose in every stage of life. She also equips individuals with tools to discuss retirement and aging with their friends and loved ones, so each person can feel fully supported during their transition to retirement. Brenda is a Financial Paraplanner Qualified Professional™ and an Accredited Portfolio Management Advisor℠. Connect with Brenda at www.linkedin.com/in/brendacarrico.

Notes

1. Julie Garber, "Here Is a Step-By-Step Guide to Opening a Probate Estate," *The Balance*, https://www.thebalance.com/step-by-step-guide-to-opening-a-probate-estate-3505260.

Deciding Where To Live In Retirement

By Susan Ackley

There are many decisions to make when you are considering retirement. That's not a surprise to anyone who has contemplated retirement. The scary thing about some retirement decisions is that they can be expensive and difficult to modify once the decision to act has been made. So thought and planning are necessary. But with so many options available, where do you begin?

I have tried to present the reader with a primer of what to consider, a lengthy list of questions to consider to work towards honing what is important to you, and a dos and don'ts list with additional and specific information.

I have two starting objectives for those considering the 'where to live in retirement' decision. They are: taking the time to look at and be aware of the myriad of options, but, most importantly, to know yourself and what you want. And don't forget your spouse or partner! If your spouse or partner isn't fully on board, count on problems ensuing.

So, the more information you have, the better you know yourself and your likes and dislikes, along with some solid planning can help make this decision making process a bit easier, but it doesn't fully eliminate of all of the angst of making such a big, potentially life altering decision.

I met Matt and Janny at an expo where I was presenting on the benefits of Retirement Coaching. They approached me afterwards with some general questions, but I could hear they had something specific they wanted to ask about.

Matt got to the point when he said that they needed some help to make a decision about where to live in retirement. As a Certified Retirement Coach, I knew that I could help them get to the core of their question through coaching.

Matt had retired two years earlier, at age 55, after a long career as an engineer for a large local manufacturer. Janny, now aged 55, was still working as a paralegal for a law firm, but she had decided to retire in six months.

Matt and Janny had grown children, both who lived in other cities. They had both grown up in the local area. They had very few family members living locally, but they had many friends living nearby and a few who had also already retired and moved to Florida, California, or Arizona.

Matt said he was ready to move somewhere that he didn't have to shovel snow. They had rented a condo for several months of the winters of the past two years near Tampa, Florida. They visited various areas south and east of Tampa and had attended many real estate open houses, but they weren't completely sold on any specific area or even what type of property they wanted. So were still indecisive.

Janny said that she wanted them to be more adventurous and to expand their search internationally. She was intrigued by what she had been reading lately about Panama. She felt that since both she and Matt were still under 60, they were too young to plant themselves in Florida for the rest of their lives.

Their adult children also weren't enamored with Tampa. Janny also found that winters weren't warm enough but summers were too hot and humid. She wanted to explore the idea of a living in Panama and starting a tourism related business there. She was sure one of their children would want to join the business, so she was very excited and thought this would give her retirement a purpose.

Research shows that the top two decisions retirees have to make is when to retire and where to live. The decision of, "Where do I live?" can be overwhelming because there are just so many choices and factors to consider.

- Do you want to stay in the same area where you live now?
- Perhaps you want to move to a smaller community?
- Do you want to live abroad?
- Perhaps you want to live on a sailboat traveling the world, closer to family, in a nearby 55-plus community, a golf community, or The Villages?
- How much should you spend on a home?

- Should we downsize or stay in our current home instead?
- Do you want a home or condominium?
- What are the taxes and expenses related to that area?
- Buy or rent?

What seems to happen is that making one decision such as the where to live, leads directly to another decision, such as what type of property to buy or how much to spend, which directly leads to another decision, and on, and on, and on.

With past generations, the primary concern for retirees deciding where to live in retirement was climate. However, financial considerations have joined with climate particularly for Baby Boomers who may be living 30 years or more in retirement and are worried about their money lasting and also leaving a legacy.

Baby Boomers today are well-traveled more than retirees of generations past. Many areas of the world have become more accessible and politically stable. Technological advances and an increase in travel options also have made us a more mobile society.

Information and access to the internet is much more reliable and readily available, and we have a greater awareness of the benefits of many more countries. The world has truly has become 'our oyster'.

In the past, retiring to international destinations wasn't viewed as a viable option unless one was extremely wealthy. But today, less expensive options are there allowing retirees to be able to retire abroad.

You can turn on HGTV and watch people house hunt across the world from the comfort of your couch. Unfortunately, living abroad does require some additional planning. But if you and your spouse are both in agreement about living abroad it can be a very satisfying option.

The U.S. is probably the most convenient country in the world, with access to anything you may want or need almost anytime you want it. That is not always true if you live abroad. Depending upon where you choose to live, shipping times can be lengthy and importation of goods can make them more expensive.

International living also requires leaving your expectations at home and learning to live with a less efficient way of getting things done. If you are a control freak, living abroad may be a very frustrating experience.

Waiting for a contractor or a home service can be especially difficult because, often, "mañana" is the way things work.

A sense of adventure and a sense of humor are necessary. Having tolerance to change and being adaptable are also required. Though after a time, you may find that you begin to adapt to the new way of living and enjoy it very much.

Having a re-entry plan back to living in the U.S. would be something to consider before deciding to live abroad. Perhaps you could rent your home for a time, or have funds set aside if you decide you want to return to the United States.

You may change your mind about being so far from friends and family. Also, as you age, your needs may change. A safety net is best to have in place.

If we look closer to home, the four most popular retirement destinations, according to the Brookings Institution, are Phoenix, AZ; Riverside, CA; Tampa and St. Petersburg, FL; and Atlanta, GA. They all have one thing in common: they are all in warm locations and they are all in the U.S.

Being a 'snowbird' is also a popular option if you live in the northern areas of the United States that experiences cold or snowy winters. This could mean spending anywhere from one to six months in a warmer location, returning to your home state in the spring.

According to USA Today, the age group of 55-and-older of Florida swells about 138% annually. Arizona has an increase of about the same number. As more and more Baby Boomers retire, those numbers will increase.[1]

However, clement weather shouldn't be the only criteria when considering retirement residence. There are many other factors to consider even if weather is a top priority for you.

Where to Start

After I met with Matt and Janny, I emailed them a homework assignment to complete before our first coaching session. The first assignment was for them each to list, in order of their preference, their top six leisure activities.

I offered this homework because I think it is important for them to think about and consider what leisure activities to narrow the field of locations. If they both love to sail the ocean, a mountain location wouldn't be ideal for them. It also gets to what is important to them.

The other questions I ask are meant to be useful towards learning more about how they want to live life in retirement, who they are, and to find overlap. If Matt wants to ski, golf, and be near big name entertainment and professional sports but Janny wants to live quietly on a ranch and staring a goat yoga business, can they both get what they want through negotiation and compromise and find a location that will suit them both?

Following is an extensive and encompassing list of questions. Try to answer as many of the following questions as you can for yourself. It may help you learn more about what you want:

- What kind of climate do you like best?
- How important is it for you to be near family?
- Do you like participating in group activities?

- How important is it for you to be near a top-notch health facility? How near is near enough?
- Are you a lover of the water?
- Do you plan to or hope to volunteer?
- Do you like lots of activity, or do you prefer to "kick back"?
- Do you want to travel? How often? Where?
- Do you have 'bucket list' items you'd like to do?
- Is accessibility to an airport important? Ideal distance?
- How important are educational opportunities close by?
- How important is it to have cultural activities nearby?
- Can you afford to live in the location of your choice?
- Are you a country boy or girl and want to live in a small community?
- Would you rather live in a college town with many opportunities to audit college classes and have young people/students nearby?
- Would you like to have the tax advantages of a 55-plus planned retirement community that provides outside home maintenance, some leisure activities and like-minded adults?
- Would you prefer to live at or near the lake or golf course? A resort destination?
- Would an international location be where you want to live? Will language be a factor?

- Do you have a housing type preference: single family home, attached townhouse, city high rise, a ranch with animals, a farm with acreage, a low-rise condo, two-story house in a neighborhood, one level home, yurt, mobile home, motor home?
- Buy or rent?

Here are additional questions to consider:

- How difficult or easy will it be for you, emotionally and psychologically, to relocate?
- If you were to relocate, what are some of the "must haves" on your list for an ideal place?
- Are you more of a person who seeks new social groups, or are you a person who craves "alone time"?
- Of all the different types of retirement communities I've listed above, which one appeals to you the most?
- Have you considered any locations and later dismissed them? Why?
- Is a move really necessary? What are the pros and cons of retiring locally or staying put in your home?
- Do you feel it necessary to downsize?
- Have you considered your housing budget?
- Do you mind driving a long distance to the doctor or grocery store?
- Is your decision based solely on the proximity to family? Is there a possibility your family may relocate in the near future?

A Few Dos And Don'ts

Do look for a lower cost of living. One of the biggest fears of many retirees is running out of money in retirement. I know I get the shivers just thinking about that possibility. I am not a financial expert but I do know the three largest outgoing expenses besides your home are health care costs, food, and utilities. So, it stands to reason that if you lower your cost of living, there will be more money for a longer time. There is a huge variation in housing costs across the country and around the world.

There are many cost of living calculators and comparisons available online. A Google search will list many such options. There are several in which it is possible to enter your current city, your current income, and the city you are considering in which to relocate and find out, across categories, the differences in cost of living.

The website Numbeo offers a cost of living index which rates global cities by cost of living. It rates New York City currently at the number 12 most expensive city in the world. Switzerland has five cities in the top six most expensive cities in the world. They also have other pages that have ratings of cities on criteria such as pollution, traffic, health care, etc. (https://www.numbeo.com/cost-of-living/rankings.jsp).

The website Best Places offers a comparison by city across consumer price categories (https://www.bestplaces.net/cost-of-living/).

USA Today offers a listing of the value of a dollar in every state in the United States (https://www.usatoday.com/story/money/economy/2018/05/10/cost-of-living-value-of-dollar-in-every-state/34567549/).

Mercer also offers an excellent online resource for cost of living data. Their rankings consider the cost of 200 goods and services that affect the cost of living (https://mobilityexchange.mercer.com/Insights/cost-of-living-rankings).

Also, you may find the US Consumer Price Index website useful for tracking changes in the Consumer Price Index (https://www.bls.gov/cpi/).

You will also see articles printed annually on the best places to live in retirement published by a myriad of magazines, newspapers, and websites. But yours is the only opinion that matters for your decision, so don't get sidetracked by media.

Besides cost of living comparisons, do look for information about population, economy, traffic, crime, attractions, and general information about considered locations via the internet.

Also, visit the location's visitor bureau, and try to talk to locals. Specific climate information is available on the National Climatic Data Center online (https://www.ncdc.noaa.gov/).

Crime rates can be researched on the FBI's annual Uniform Crime Reports (https://ucr.fbi.gov/). Health care reports online can be searched online for a Guide to the Best Hospitals with a database that can be searched by location and specialty.

Do consider immigration issues if you are thinking of retiring internationally. The ability to get a residency permit may be difficult and expensive. You don't want to have to leave the country for three months every three months if you only have a 90 day visitor visa. You may also not be able to work or earn money if you are do not have the correct immigration status. Consult the consulate of the country you are considering to live for more information and rules and regulations.

Do look for states that offer tax breaks for retiree residents. There are several state tax comparison charts that allow you to view income, sales, and property tax by state. For example, Mississippi doesn't tax retirement income and the first $75,000 of a personal residence value is exempt from property taxes for those over 65. Florida, Texas, and Washington have no state income tax. But don't move solely for state income taxes, or as my mother used to say to my father when he worried about income taxes, "you're letting the tax tail wag the dog" (https://www.aarp.org/livable-communities/network-age-friendly-communities/).

Retirement can mean you have transitioned to a fixed income with less flexibility, so a location with a higher cost of living can squeeze the budget and a location with a lower cost of living can ease the squeeze.

If your income is fixed and you are over age 62, another consideration is to look at governmental or community senior housing options. There can be income limits but, if you qualify, rent is typically 30% of your income and often includes utilities. Be aware there could be a lengthy wait list.

The website After55.com is a useful resource for learning more about low income housing options (https://www.after55.com/blog/how-find-low-income-senior-housing/). Your local Sunday newspaper may also have information on your local senior communities and rentals. Contacting your local Area Agency on Aging or senior social services can be a useful and informative resource.

Do check into any association or planned community in which you are considering purchasing. Ask to see the by-laws for rules and restrictions, and copies of recent community financials and any special assessments. You can also ask a local real estate agent who may know about management, what is included in the assessment, and what amenities and services are available. If the community doesn't have a website or Facebook page consider that how open communication could be limited, which isn't ideal.

Do ask about the board of directors and how long the directors have been in office and term lengths (more than two terms is too long), or if residents are hesitant to serve as directors. A tyrannical board president or incompetent manager can make life difficult for residents. Ask if rentals are allowed, and consider renting to experience life in that community before buying. The Villages in Florida is an example of a community that offers rentals to try before buying.

Do find a purpose for yourself. We all need a reason to get out of bed in the morning. Take up a long-deferred hobby, try learning a new language, volunteer, teach a skill to a child, start a small business, get a part-time job, play a sport, learn something new, for example. You can do any of these no matter where you retire and purpose can help you feel like more a part of your community and fulfilled and happy.

Don't forget to consider that your life can bring change and loss and you may want or need to modify your living situation should health or life circumstances change or you just change your mind. Plan an exit strategy and segregate the money in an exit fund so you can quickly set an exit in motion.

Don't base your decision solely on the proximity to family. Children grow up and move away, adult children can relocate because of jobs. You could also become a built-in babysitter and your family may want to overtake all your free time. You may have to set some boundaries with them if they do.

Don't allow yourself to become isolated no matter where you retire. No matter where you are living, as you age, you need to have a balance of alone time and socialization. You will live longer and be happier.

Do find a way to entertain yourself that doesn't involve the television, computer, or video games. Screen time is not always quality time.

What about Matt and Janny?

Matt and Janny had now coached with me for three months. They had productively spent time researching their decision of where to live in retirement. They each had their own epiphanies about what they wanted in a retirement location and home. These required negotiation and compromise on both sides, but both were open to this.

They had taken a six-week trip to Panama, trying to live as much like locals as possible. However, after the trip, Panama had lost its charm as their ideal place for their lives in retirement, especially for Matt. However, they have both agreed to continue to research locations in the Caribbean and also added Spain to their list.

I would consider this good news for them. They are working on making an informed decision based on what they both want and need, and are taking the time to figure out their next step. They thought the decision would come more quickly, but they have grown in the process and realize "… it will take as long as it takes".

For now, they have decided that they will list their home for sale and sell off or give away several rooms of furniture and other items once Janny retires. They have contacted a real estate broker and are looking to buy a well-located, two bedroom condo locally to use as a home base from which to travel extensively. Janny also realized that it would be helpful to have an address in the U.S. and a place to come back to as part of a re-entry plan, if they do decide to live internationally.

Matt and Janny seem to have fully embraced their new adventure and are very excited. Janny, in a moment of honest clarity, told me, "I'm not sure where we will finally end up living, and it could even be Florida, but for now, I want to travel and see what else the world has to offer and where I fit in."

They have decided to continue coaching with me to help them in their transition. They emailed me recently stating "We appreciate your perspective and the support that you give us. If we hadn't met you, we would either be stuck here fighting it, living miserably in Panama, or headed for divorce court."

So you can see that making the decision of where to live in retirement isn't easy or one that can be or should be made quickly. Matt and Janny's interim decision confirmed the difficulty in making a decision of where to live in retirement is. Their conclusion that they needed more time and information fits their needs.

No matter how you decide or what process you go through to get to the decision of where to live in retirement, please know yourself well and take your time to find a good fit for you and your spouse or partner.

Even if your decision is to stay in your current home and travel to warmer locations for winters, or buy a second home, if your finances allow, that may be sounder than making a decision in haste and regretting it in leisure.

If you use the resources I've included, you should have a good start towards learning more about yourself and what is important to you, and be able to move you closer towards your objective.

Please start thinking about and completing the questions honestly and in some depth. If what you learn isn't enough to move you closer towards a decision, find a Certified Retirement Coach to work with to help you find your own unique and individual answers.

Either way, I know that you will see that the time and energy you expend will be well worth the effort to help you towards finding where to live in retirement. Although it may end up being a hybrid of what you had originally expected.

About The Author

Susan Ackley considers herself to be a Retirement Activist, with a strong aspiration to expand knowledge about and the impact of Retirement Coaching worldwide. She is passionate about helping retiring Baby Boomers find direction and fulfillment through self-knowledge and retirement coaching. She is a Certified Retirement Coach and founding member of the Retirement Coaches Association. She is also a Licensed Mental Health and Addictions Counselor. Susan lives with her husband, and their energetic Wheaten Terrier, in a 55 plus community near Chicago, Illinois. They are searching for their ideal warm weather spot to someday flee snowy Midwest winters. Visit www.findretirementdirection.com

Notes

1. Tim Henderson, "Retirement Moves Make a Comeback," *USA Today*, June 16, 2014, https://www.usatoday.com/story/money/person alfinance/2014/06/16/stateline-retirement-moving/10575961/.

Design Your Best Retirement

By Joan Lambert

As you probably know, people are living longer than at any time in human history. Some of us will leave our full-time jobs and, if we are lucky, have another three decades in good health. Some who retire early could have even more time.

A few fortunate people know exactly what they want to do once they retire, and have no problem implementing their plan. If you are one of those fortunate few, you probably could skip ahead. This chapter is for the rest of us!

It can be challenging to figure out how to spend your time once you are done with full-time work (or parenting).[1] How much time should be spent relaxing, pursuing meaningful or challenging activities, alone or with others, at home, or traveling?

There is no one-size-fits-all retirement plan. I'll discuss some of the latest research in this area to get you thinking and show you how to apply Design Thinking concepts, so you can stay fulfilled throughout your life.

Risks of Isolating Yourself

I'm one of those people who obsessively researches everything, so when I wanted to prepare for becoming an "empty-nester" and a new job coaching people as they move into retirement, I spent considerable time reviewing the research.[2] I quickly realized that the research is not in dispute: People who engage in meaningful activities and forge strong connections with other people live happier, healthier and longer lives.

This may sound obvious, but what was not obvious were the risks associated with not doing these things. Studies have now shown that socially isolated people face serious health risks. In fact, experts have learned that isolation can literally kill you.

For example, in one study done at Stanford University, researchers concluded that socially isolated people face health risks comparable to those of smokers.[3] In addition, their mortality risk is two times greater than that of obese people.

As if that wasn't alarming enough, an additional concern is that those 55-64 years old are less likely to be socially engaged than people of that age in previous generations. This study finds that, "[t]his age group, part of the Baby Boom generation, are less likely to have meaningful interactions with a spouse or partner."

They also have weaker ties to family, friends, and neighbors, and are less likely to engage in church and other community activities than those who were the same age 20 years ago.

Many other studies have also shown that social isolation is bad for your health and that having good social relationships can help people live longer. One "meta" study analyzed data from 148 different studies with a total of over 300,000 people who were followed for an average of 7.5 years.

The results indicated that people with good social relationships have a 50% reduced risk of early death compared to those with poor social relationships, an effect similar to quitting smoking.[4]

This study shows that the magnitude of effect of having good social relationships is not only comparable with quitting smoking, but "it exceeds many well-known risk factors for mortality (e.g., obesity, physical inactivity)."

Therefore, when planning what to do in retirement, make sure to include activities where you interact with other people on a regular basis so you don't become isolated.

The Importance of Feeling Useful

In addition to staying socially connected, we all need to feel useful. One study of people in their 70s in several cities across the United States shows that feeling useful to others as we age is critical.[5]

This study shows that a persistently high level of feeling useful to others is associated with a significantly lower risk of death. Conversely, people with persistently low feelings of usefulness or who experienced a decline in feelings of usefulness during the three-year course of the study, experienced a greater likelihood of dying. This need to feel useful as we age, is not limited to the United States. A study from China found comparable results.[6] While we are working full time, we generally feel useful and that we are contributing to society.

This applies to full-time caregiving as well. When my daughters were young, I left a career as a lawyer, and spent part of their childhood working part time or staying home and volunteering. During this period, I felt I was doing something useful.

However, once I contemplated no longer working or raising a family, I worried about no longer feeling "useful." As a result, I started doing a lot of volunteering, and eventually served on several nonprofit boards and as an elected member of a local public school board.

Volunteering helped me feel useful even though I wasn't working at a traditional job. As I later learned, research consistently indicates that volunteering confers enormous mental and physical benefits to those who volunteer. And those benefits are especially potent for those who volunteer later in life.

In a study done by the MacArthur Foundation Research Network on an Aging Society, researchers found that volunteering in later life is associated with a reduced risk of hypertension, higher well-being, better cognition and lower mortality.[7]

And it appears that volunteering can actually reduce your risk of developing dementia. A Swedish study found that those who volunteer in later life have lower self-reported cognitive complaints and a lower risk for dementia, relative to those who do not volunteer, or only volunteer sporadically.[8]

Finally, an Irish study found that the positive association between volunteer work and well-being is widely documented.[9] This study showed that volunteer work leads to better self-reported health, higher life satisfaction, and decreased rates of depression. Further, the lowest quality of life was found for people who never volunteer, regardless of their age.

Clearly many people derive a lot of satisfaction from volunteering, but if you don't volunteer you can obtain similar benefits as long as you engage in activities you find meaningful.

One study of older Los Angeles residents used something called the "Meaningful Activity Participation Assessment" (MAPA), where people indicated their participation in and the degree of personal meaningfulness they felt while doing 28 different typical activities.

This study suggests that participating in activities having greater personal significance may have more influence upon well-being and quality of life than participation in a greater number of activities that are less personally significant.[10] So while it might sound obvious, think about how you spend your time, and how much time you spend doing activities that are really meaningful to you. If you can increase time spent on meaningful activities, you're likely to be happier.

In addition, to staying socially connected and feeling useful through activities that are meaningful, try to have multiple "roles" during retirement. Research shows that people who do multiple "roles" fare better as they age.

For example, one study showed that among older adults, people had a higher degree of reported well-being when they had multiple roles instead of just one. For example, people reported better health when they did more than one of the following roles: caregiving, paid work, irregular work, volunteering, or informal social assistance.[11]

So, if you can arrange your life to engage in various roles after you leave full-time work, you are likely to be more content.

Intro to Design Thinking

As we just saw, research strongly suggests that if you can do the following things you'll have a more fulfilled retirement:

1. Stay connected socially
2. Do activities that are personally meaningful and where you feel useful
3. Engage in multiple roles, not just one

Now that you know what the research says, let's look at how you can use it to improve your day-to-day life.

After all, just knowing the research isn't enough — you have to apply it to your life for any benefit. And, as anyone who has tried to quit a bad habit knows, changing your behavior can be difficult.

There is a whole genre of books about how to improve your life. A comprehensive look at all the methods out there is beyond the scope of this chapter, but I've found one method that has helped me, and other people, in solving problems, including the "problem" of what to do in retirement.

It's called Design Thinking, and with a few exercises using the basic steps, it can be the catalyst many people need to figure out what to do next with their lives.

You may have heard of Design Thinking, which has become a kind of "buzzword" in business, especially in Silicon Valley, where I live. The origins of Design Thinking were in the 1960s, but in the last decade or so, brothers David and Tom Kelley, founders of the consulting firm IDEO, in Palo Alto, CA, have popularized Design Thinking and used it to help their clients design products, many of which are household names.[12]

They also founded IDEO U, an online school where they and their colleagues teach the fundamentals of Design Thinking to anyone who is interested.[13]

Many colleges have also embraced Design Thinking. Stanford University, just down the street from IDEO in Palo Alto, is possibly the best known. At Stanford's "d.school" (the "d" is for Design), one of the most popular classes is a Design Thinking class where students use the methods they are taught to solve thorny problems in the world, often called "wicked" problems.

Stanford also has a year-long program, the Distinguished Careers Institute, where about 25 people who have finished their careers are chosen each year as "fellows."

These people come each year to Stanford, taking classes, and trying to figure out what to do next. A popular class is the one on Design Thinking. Harvard University has also pioneered a program similar to Stanford's, the Harvard Advanced Leadership Program.

Most of us can't uproot our lives and spend an entire year at Stanford or Harvard, not to mention afford the steep tuition for these programs. But anyone can learn how to apply Design Thinking concepts to figuring out how to best live their life.

I learned how to use Design Thinking while serving on the board of the Menlo Park City School District, where my children attended school. Our superintendent advocates using Design Thinking to solve all kinds of problems and our school district is fortunate to be a partner with Stanford's d.school in applying Design Thinking to public education. All our district's administrators have received training through Stanford.

Our school district has used Design Thinking to create a new report card, design a new bell schedule at our middle school, and develop our World Language program, among other things.

The concepts behind Design Thinking are not difficult. In fact, our district's teachers have successfully taught these concepts to students as young as elementary school!

While Design Thinking may sound like something complicated, at its core, Design Thinking is just a process for creative problem-solving that can be modified to apply to any "problem." So, if the general "problem" you are trying to solve is what to do next with your life, or how to spend your time in retirement, you can use Design Thinking to help you.

'Design' Your Way To Your Ideal Life In Retirement

Although there are some general "steps" in Design Thinking, there's no official guidebook, and no right or wrong way to "design" your life. So, experiment and find what works for you. And if you aren't sure if this whole Design Thinking idea is for you, that's OK.

To be honest, I wasn't sure when I first heard about it. But after seeing how well the process worked with issues we wanted to solve in our community's schools, I realized the same concepts could work for different types of problems. Even if you're skeptical, I encourage you to take a few minutes to read the rest of the chapter and do the exercises. You can do the exercises alone or with others.

If you have a spouse or partner, it can spark great conversations to do the exercises together. You can also do them with a friend, or a small group of friends.

There are slightly different methodologies in Design Thinking, but I'm going to explain the steps used by the Stanford d.school and tweak them a bit so they work for our purposes.

If you are interested in a more in-depth look at how to use Design Thinking in your life, a wonderful book is *Designing Your Life* by Bill Burnett and Dave Evans, two professors who teach the popular Stanford class on the same subject.[14]

Their book is comprehensive and gives many examples and exercises on how to use Design Thinking to guide your life. Although most of the examples in the book are about people in the early or middle stages of their career, the techniques in the book can be used at any stage of life.

The basic steps of Design Thinking are: Empathize, Define, Ideate, Prototype, and Test. Here's a short explanation of each step and exercises you can do to apply them in your life.

Empathize

Typically, in this step you try to understand the people for whom you are designing (since most problems also involve other people). Normally, you would interview these people.

In our case, you don't need to interview yourself, but during this step, you should think about how you spend your time, how much time you have available for new activities, and what is important and meaningful to you. One way to do this is to do a time assessment or time diary. You don't need any fancy tools to do this.

For the most accurate picture, think about a typical week and write down how you spend your time each day. You can use a chart to do this, or just use a separate sheet of paper. Try to be as accurate as possible. This time chart is just for you and you don't need to show this to anyone else.

Once you're done, think about how much of your time is spent doing activities that are meaningful to you and how much time you spend on other things.

Many people are surprised at how much time they spend doing things that are not very meaningful. Also, many people are shocked to realize how much time they spend online. According to a Pew Research Center survey, in January 2018, 26% of American adults now report that they go online "almost constantly" and 43% say they go online several times a day.[15]

Look at your time chart and think about how much time you have available if you wanted to add new activities. How much time would you want to use each week for something new? Once you know this, go on to the next step.

Exercise: Create a time chart of what you do each day. Once you are done, look at how you use your time and whether you have some time that could be used each week to do something more meaningful.

You can do this on the computer, or simply take a sheet of paper and make a list each day for a week.

Include the following:

- Day/Time spent

- Activity

- Meaningfulness of activity (e.g., none, low, medium, high)

For a fun and interactive way to do a time chart online, go to Amava.com and fill out your Engagement Assessment. (Full disclosure: this is the company I work for and you'll need to create a free account.)

Define

During this phase, you will define the problem you are trying to solve. For our purposes, the important thing is to define an actionable problem statement. This is harder than it sounds. It's important to be broad and not focus too much on a specific solution. But at the same time, your problem must be also narrow enough that it is actionable.

For example, a problem statement of "improve my life" or "do more meaningful things" would be too broad. In fact, crafting a more narrowly focused problem statement often results in better solutions when you are generating ideas in the next step. If you're not sure how to do this, just take a stab at it. You can always go back and refine it later.

If you are trying to figure out what to do next, your "problem" statement could be something concrete such as: "I'd like to find a part-time volunteer position where I can work with animals."

Or it could be more general, such as: "I want to find something to do where I can help kids." There is no right or wrong answer here. Think about something you would like to change in your life and draft a "problem" statement.

Exercise: Write down a "problem" you would like to solve in your life. If you aren't sure, you can write down a few different options and pick one to start with, and then go back and pick another after completing the exercises.

Ideate

Ideation is the step of the design process in which you come up with lots of ideas.

Think of it as a process of "going wide" in terms of possible solutions. Ideation can also be thought of as brainstorming. Sometimes this is also referred to as "flaring," because the idea is to generate as many ideas as possible during this phase. During this process, be creative and write down whatever you think of. Wild ideas are OK. Don't worry if your ideas seem silly or farfetched. In this stage, let your imagination take over and write down anything that comes into your mind as a possible solution to your problem. One way to do this is to think about "how might I ..." questions.

Exercise: Think about your "problem" and write down as many solutions to the problem as you can think of. Go for quantity, not quality. You'll narrow them down in the next step.

Prototype

When designing in business, a prototype is often a physical object like a product. In this case, though there is no physical object you are creating so the prototypes will be ideas and actions, not objects.

To start, take all the ideas you generated from your "ideate" list and narrow them down. One simple way to do this is to decide on the three or four best ideas from your list. For each of these ideas, think about how you can test the idea without investing a lot of time and money up front.

How you do that is a "prototype." In other words, for each of the ideas, think about how you can take a small step to try out your idea. In *Designing Your Life*, the authors explain how to prototype something you want to do. They recommend doing interviews with people who are doing what you are interested in, which they call "Life Design Interviews." They also recommend finding a mentor who can help you.

Exercise: Take each of your three or four ideas and talk to someone about how to do it. For example, if you want to take a Spanish class, call a local community college and find out what classes are available. See if you can sit in on one class for a day.

Or, if you want to find a volunteer position working with children, call your local school district and find out what opportunities are available. See if you can spend an hour or two observing others who are volunteering.

In this step, try to find a way to try out the activity you think you want to do. This could be a paid or volunteer job, a class, or anything else you might want to do.

Test

Now that you've done your prototype, figure out which one you want to do first. It can be easier to start with something small. You don't need to change your entire life. Find one thing you want to do — like a new activity each week.

Don't worry if you aren't sure that what you are doing is right. Start by taking a step. Have a bias to action. If you try something and you don't like it, you can stop and try something else. Don't worry too much about analyzing or wondering if you are doing the right thing.

Exercise: Pick one of the scenarios you came up to prototype and figure out how to do it on a longer-term basis. For example, if you want to learn a new language, go ahead and actually sign up for lessons or a class. If you want to write your memoir, find a creative writing group to join. Finding a new activity is usually fairly straightforward to do, especially if you've already researched it.

However, if you are wanting to make a bigger change, like transition into a new encore career, then it could require more preparation and a longer time to implement. For some people, if you can start with a small activity or action, you can then "work your way up" to tackle a bigger challenge.

Hopefully after seeing the research and doing these exercises where you use Design Thinking — you can take some actions toward a more fulfilling life. No matter your age, it's never too late to create a life you love!

About The Author

Joan Lambert leads research and helps members design their next chapters at Amava (www.amava.com), an organization dedicated to keeping people active and connected throughout their lives. Joan also mentors first-generation college students and is finishing her eighth year as an elected trustee on the board of the Menlo Park City School District. Previously, Joan served on several non-profit boards in Seattle and the Bay Area, and co-founded the Preeclampsia Foundation, after a career practicing law in California and New York. Joan holds a JD from UCLA and a BA in English from UC Berkeley.

Notes

1. Although I use the word "retirement", the concepts in this chapter are equally applicable to people who have been out of the workforce while raising children and are now "empty-nesters."

2. See *The Paradox of Choice: Why More is Less* (Barry Schwartz, New York: Ecco, 2016), for a good discussion of why narrowing down choices can greatly reduce the stress, anxiety, and busyness of our lives, and why too many choices can result in "analysis paralysis."

3. *The Sightlines Project: Seeing Our Way to Living Long, Living Well in 21st Century America*, Stanford University, http://longevity.stanford.edu/wp-content/uploads/2017/06/Sightlines-Project-FINAL_1-9-2017.pdf

4. Julianne Holt-Lunstad, Timothy Smith, and J. Layton, "Social Relationships and Mortality Risk: A Meta-analytic Review," *PLOS Medicine*, 2010, http://journals.plos.org/plosmedicine/article?id=10.1371/journal.pmed.1000316.

5. Tara L. Gruenewald et al., "Increased Mortality Risk in Older Adults With Persistently Low or Declining Feelings of Usefulness to Others," *Journal of Aging and Health* 21, no. 2 (2009), https://www.ncbi.nlm.nih.gov/pmc/articles/PMC2747376/

6. Yuan Zhao et al., "Changes in Perceived Uselessness and Risks for Mortality: Evidence from a National Sample of Older Adults in China," *BMC Public Health* 17, no. 1 (2017), https://www.ncbi.nlm.nih.gov/pubmed/28599631

7. Dawn C. Carr, Linda P. Fried, and John W. Rowe, "Productivity & Engagement in an Aging America: The Role of Volunteerism," *Daedalus* 144, no. 2 (2015), https://www.mitpressjournals.org/doi/abs/10.1162/DAED_a_00330?journalCode=daed#.WNv9eCMrK9Y

8. Yannick Griep, et al., "Can Volunteering in Later Life Reduce the Risk of Dementia? A 5-year Longitudinal Study among Volunteering and Non-volunteering Retired Seniors," *Plos One* 12, no. 3 (2017), https://www.ncbi.nlm.nih.gov/pmc/articles/PMC5354395/

9. Christine McGarrigle, et al., "Health and Wellbeing: Active Ageing for Older Adults in Ireland," The Irish Longitudinal Study on Ageing (2017), see http://tilda.tcd.ie/; and https://tilda.tcd.ie/publications/reports/pdf/w3-key-findings-report/TILDA%20Wave%203%20Key%20Findings%20report.pdf

10. Aaron M. Eakman, Mike E. Carlson, and Florence A. Clark, "The Meaningful Activity Participation Assessment: A Measure of Engagement in Personally Valued Activities," *The International Journal of Aging and Human Development* 70, no. 4 (2010), https://www.ncbi.nlm.nih.gov/pmc/articles/PMC3177298/

11. James E. Hinterlong, Nancy Morrow-Howell, and Philip A. Rozario, "Productive Engagement and Late Life Physical and Mental Health," *Research on Aging* 29, no. 4 (2007), https://www.researchgate.net/publication/240691084_Productive_Engagement_and_Late_Life_Physical_and_Mental_Health_Findings_from_a_Nationally_Representative_Panel_Study

12. Visit https://www.ideo.com/search?tags=Products for some of the products IDEO has helped to design.

13. Visit https://www.ideou.com/ for information about the courses offered.

14. William Burnett and David J. Evans, *Designing Your Life: How to Build a Well-lived, Joyful Life* (New York: Alfred A. Knopf, 2017).

15. Andrew Perrin and Jingjing Jiang, "About a Quarter of U.S. Adults Say They Are 'Almost Constantly' Online," *Pew Research Center*, March 14, 2018, http://www.pewresearch.org/fact-tank/2018/03/14/about-a-quarter-of-americans-report-going-online-almost-constantly/.

Living Younger Longer: Increase Your Healthspan

By Joel Shuflin

There's no doubt that the second half of life is getting to be a longer stretch — recent estimates from the actuarial-types indicate that every year, those born have at least a 6-month-longer lifespan than those born the previous year, in great part because of breakthroughs in medical discoveries that are extending the life of people with illnesses that once meant quick death: cancers, leukemia and even diabetes.

Currently, the expected lifespan (years of living) for Americans is an average of about 80 years (slightly more for women, slightly less for men. If we actually make it to age 65, the statisticians are willing to give us till 85. (Gee, thanks!)

That's average.

Just because we're living longer, doesn't mean that we're living well during those extra months and years. In fact, many of us aren't. The breakthroughs in medicine and treatment that save lives don't necessarily restore a vital, healthy life.

For example, a friend of mine just went through a successful round of chemotherapy for very advanced colon cancer that had metastasized into his liver. Frankly, I thought he might not make it more than a few weeks into the treatment. One year later he's currently free of any tumors — but he's not healthy. There are a host of side-effects of the treatment, and the likelihood that he'll be taking some sort of maintenance-level chemo for the rest of his life.

That's why the senior care market (including assisted-living and in-home care) is booming at an annual compound rate of 8 percent.[1] That's also why Medicare is at risk of running out of money.

By 2060, there will be close to 100 million Americans over 65, and the average ones won't be all that healthy.[2] Consider this:

- The average American 65 and older has 19 prescriptions in a year (under 65, the average is 12)

- 94% of Americans over 65 are taking medication to control high blood pressure

- The cost of healthcare for someone over 65 is 3-5 times higher than someone under 65

- Two out of 3 Americans over 65 have multiple chronic conditions (heart disease, lower respiratory disease, diabetes, influenza, Alzheimer's, cancer)

- The average American over 50 reports having 5 days per month in which they have some "limits on their activity" because of health

And yet, amazingly about 75% of these same people report that they think they are in good health!

Who wants to be average?

Certainly not me, and I'm betting not you! That's one reason why you're reading this book! You're already doing something that isn't average: You're taking steps to intentionally design the second half of your life.

Here's the challenge: Every day, the Internet spin cycle spits out new articles and advertisements for this cure, that supplement, and yet another veritable "fountain of youth" pill, or a celebrity pushing the health transforming effects of something along the likes of cockroach milk.[3]

Yes, you read that right. Cockroach milk is the latest fad superfood!

I'm sure by the time you're reading this, there will be dozens of new ones. You could spend a lot of time and a small fortune trying them all. There's no doubt that many fads prove to be valuable — and they graduate from passing fad to mainstream fact.

Rather than try to chase after the latest and greatest, a more practical approach is to pick one or two simple, proven, and easy-to-do solutions and pursue them regularly.

And that, finally, is the optimism you've been waiting to hear: You don't have to be average.

It's not too late to start being above average

It's true: When it comes to your health, you can improve your future prospects, no matter when you start. Researchers from Harvard, Yale, Tufts, and the Medical University of South Carolina found that a shift in health habits late in life (that means over 45) has not only an immediate effect on well-being, but also sustained benefits over time.[4]

In a Johns Hopkins-led study which tracked more than 6,000 people ages 44 to 84 for more than seven years, those who made positive healthy habit changes decreased their risk of death in the span by 80%.[5]

Chances are you know exactly what your unhealthy habits are (or have been). I'm betting they're not too unlike some of mine.

The Seven Unhealthy Sins

1. Consuming food prepared in vegetable oils (including chips, crackers, French fries, popcorn, chicken with any kind of crust, anything baked in a factory, salad dressings, desserts such as puddings, and ice cream).

2. Eating less than 4 cups a day of raw vegetables and fruit.

3. Eating less than 1-1.5 pounds of wild-caught deep-sea fish or salmon each week.

4. Exercising less than 75 minutes each week.

5. Exercising and feeding your brain less than daily.

6. Sleeping soundly less than 6-8 hours each night.

7. Never taking any supplements regularly, or, if you do — paying less attention to quality than you do to price.

I can already hear the questions and objections:

- "What? Sleeping soundly is a habit? Dude, my restless nights are out of my control!"

- "A whole pound of fish? And not the Friday fish fry?"

- "But, I only eat organic chips and crackers baked in sunflower oil!"

- "Who can eat four cups of veggies and fruit every day besides rabbits?"

There really are a few very important things that you can focus on that will increase your vitality and help you live younger longer. Here are what I believe to be the two essentials. (And here's the fine print disclaimer: I'm not your doctor. Nothing here is given as medical advice. Don't do anything to radically shift your eating habits without the advice of a licensed professional or your doctor. Always ask, "Is there any reason why I can't do this?")

The Shoestrings of Life

Remember when your shoes outlasted your shoelaces? I do. I can still picture my Chuck Taylor high tops, freshly cleaned from going in the laundry with the clothes, but with shoe laces that were starting to fray. Those little plastic tips on the ends of the shoelaces would inevitably wear out and the whole string would be at risk, getting so fuzzy on the end that lacing the top three holes was impossible.

It turns out that within our DNA, there are structures called telomeres that are a lot like the plastic ends on shoestrings. These telomeres get shorter as we grow older, and when they get too short, there's trouble. (Remember my frayed shoestring?) Short telomeres are associated with all kinds of negative aging processes which impact not only our lifespan, but our healthspan.[6]

In 2009, Dr. Elizabeth Blackburn won the Nobel Prize for her discovery of telomerase, the enzyme that replenishes telomeres — biomarkers since called the greatest predictors of longevity. Since then, she's been researching how diet, exercise and other good lifestyle habits positively influence telomeres, and therefore our healthspan.[7]

And one of the key things that Blackburn has discovered is that polyphenols are very important to slowing the natural shrinking of those tip-of-the-shoelace telomeres. Polyphenols are turning out to be some of the most important of the antioxidants that we hear about. These days, antioxidants are touted in just about every packaged food, but the antioxidants that seem to matter most in slowing down cellular aging aren't going to be found in a box of cereal with dried blueberries.

Unfortunately, the highest-polyphenol foods are not going to be found in most people's produce departments year-round. When was the last time you saw chokeberry? Here are the top 10:

- Black elderberry

- Black chokeberry

- Black currant

- High bush blueberry

- Globe artichoke heads

- Coffee

- Lowbush blueberry

- Sweet cherry

- Strawberry

- Blackberry

All seasonal for most of us, except coffee.

Coffee! Woohoo! (Just remember, the rest of the ingredients in your caramel latte frappe-*whatchamacallit*-chino are *not* healthy!)

The good news is that there are supplements that provide these polyphenols, and do so in concentrations that far exceed what we can get from any normal, balanced intake of these fruits.[8] Researchers found that those who took these supplements for at least 5 years had a 40% lower rate of telomere shortening across the adult age range compared to a healthy control group. To put this in citizen terms: An 80-year-old user of these supplements would have the same telomere length as a healthy 41-year-old.[9]

Besides polyphenol-rich foods, Blackburn has discovered that stress reduction, meditation, and exercise can also slow down the shortening of telomeres. Let's be clear here: Slowing the shortening of telomeres means that you're slowing down a key aging process at the cellular level. That's incredibly important, because if you slow down the aging processes, you'll increase your healthspan. You will, in other words, live younger longer.

Action Step 1: Take Care of Your Telomeres

How? Through exercise, daily quiet times and polyphenol-rich foods and supplements.

The Snack Attack

Back in the early 1980s, a video game came out for the Apple II computer that looked, played and even sounded an awful lot like Pac-Man, which had come out two years earlier. In both of those games, little munching characters chomp away at everything while the player tries to avoid them. Well, the attack is back: Snack foods are chomping away at our health. The worse news is that we don't know enough to run away!

240

As I was going down the aisles of the local grocery, I turned into the area where the crackers and chips are. In my particular grocery, all the "good" organic and gluten free items are on the same aisle as the regular items in that same category, except they are sectioned off and highlighted with nice green signs and labels. (Green = good, after all.) There they were, snacks that I was being told I could eat without fear of bad health implications — the organic Cheetos, Cheez-It lookalikes, and organic gluten-free versions of Ritz.

I'm not sure that organic origins make a big difference after corn has been mushed, cooked, puffed, and baked on a conveyor belt and sprayed with ("real") dehydrated white cheddar powder. I do believe, however, that the most insidious part of all of these snacks is the vegetable oil with which they are mixed, fried or baked. What's the reason? Vegetable oils are loaded with Omega-6 fatty acids (as are some other fun foods like salad dressings, mayo, beef, and pork).

The key detriment of all these Omega-6 fatty acids is that our body needs a balanced ratio of Omega-6 to Omega-3, and in our average Western diet, that ration is grossly out of whack. The National Institute of Health reports that humans evolved to support a 1-1 ratio, and that having a 3-1 ratio (Omega-6 to Omega-3) would be good. The average Western diet creates ratios closer to 20 to 1!

That has happened because we get fewer Omega-3s in our diet, and we're getting way more Omega-

6s than we can handle, primarily through vegetable oils.

The NIH warns that this imbalance is directly linked to all kinds of chronic diseases "including cardiovascular disease, cancer, and inflammatory and autoimmune diseases" and that correcting the balance can have significant positive effects for these diseases as well as arthritis, asthma, and other chronic conditions.[10]

It's common knowledge that Omega-3s come in abundance in cold-water fish (not just *any* fish) such as North Atlantic Cod or Salmon. To get what the experts consider enough Omega-3s, we need to eat about a pound and a half of Omega-3-rich fish each week. For vegans, the challenge is even greater in that Omega-3s are not as dense in plant sources. This is one nutritional area where supplementation is almost a must, unless you're eating the right fish daily.

There are dozens of Omega-3 supplements available, but the best ones are micro-distilled to eliminate any potential contaminants from fish (such as mercury), are cold processed from sustainable fish species, and are caught using methods that don't trap and kill dolphins and other creatures. The less expensive ones will use a combination of lower-grade fish oils and often cause burps that smell like a pond.

Now you might be asking (like I did, when I first learned this), "Can't I just get my Omega-6 —

Omega-3 balance by popping more Omega-3 capsules?" Well, no. Getting the balance is going to require cutting back on Omega-6-laden snacks and foods and supplementing with Omega-3.

Action Step #2: Get Omegas In Balance

How? By swapping out raw veggies for crackers and chips, eating fish (or Omega-3-rich vegan foods) weekly, and taking a high-quality daily Omega-3 supplement.

It's in Your Head

Now you have two areas of focus and two action steps. Seriously, that's it — just two. Right now, that's probably all you can handle, because we're not talking about trying something out. This is about making a shift that's going to enable you to have a longer healthspan during the second half of your life — to live younger longer.

How Will You Turn These Into Habits That Will Increase Your Healthspan?

Remember my unhealthy habit list? I know you're doing at least one, and probably two or more of them. We all have done them and many of us continue to do them, although we know we shouldn't. Like me and just about every other honest human being on the planet, you've tried implementing one or more of these healthy habits, but with minimal success. You've started countless times to exercise, eat right, and do crossword puzzles or other brain exercises. You've tapered off just as many times and slipped back into mindless munching of chips and salsa, crackers and cheese, or — on your best days — veggies in ranch dressing.

That brings us to the big question: "I already know that I should kick these habits, so why don't I?"

Is Your Desire Bigger Than Your Bad Habits?

Do you remember your first crush — your first love? I do. There's no one quite as motivated as a 13-year-old boy on the path to his first kiss. I had plans, I had flowers, I had messages, I had messengers, and I had the patience to try and try again. I pushed past teasing friends, frowning adults, and my own fear of failure.

My desire was strong, so was my commitment. My desire was massive, so was my action.

As you design the second half of your life, you're mapping out what you want to do, places you want to go, people you want to be with. You have big plans, fueled by desire. Stoke that desire and let that fire fuel your commitment and action that will help ensure you are healthy enough to do — and go — and be with those important people.

Become Obsessed With

My mentor, John C. Maxwell, has two favorite sayings that are both relevant here. The first is that "everything worthwhile is uphill."

That means you must make the choice to go and get it. You must put one foot in front of the other and take that journey. You must grow and stretch yourself a little every day. You may not conquer a mountain at first, but for every hill you do conquer, you gain confidence for the next climb. And there is always another hill to start climbing from the bottom. [11]

Are You Willing To Get Help?

Maxwell also says, "No one succeeds alone," and there is no reason for you to tackle the task of creating new habits all on your own. Gather around you positive, optimistic, and dedicated people who will cheer you on. Eliminate from your sphere of influence the people and voices that will hold you back or lead you away from your desires.

Consider this: You haven't yet developed all the habits you need for a healthy lifespan. Your current thinking and your current resources have gotten you to where you are today. So, it stands to reason that you may need to bring in some thinking and some outside help.

That's the tremendous value of a coach, who can enter into an alliance with you — not to tell you what steps to take, but to help you change your thinking, eliminate your limiting beliefs, and enlarge your image of your potential.

By the Way

Because I hate to leave you talking to this book saying "Those aren't two steps! That's more like five!" I want to tell you why I said two and you need to think two. I firmly believe that aside from a few exceptional people, most of us can't handle long top-level lists. We can, on the other hand, tackle a short list, even if each item on the list has sub-tasks. So focus on these two things:

1. Take Care of Your Telomeres

2. Get Your Omegas in Balance

If you do that, you'll find that you're eating better, and exercising more regularly. You'll also be slowing some of the aging process, increasing your vitality and improving your healthspan. You'll start living younger longer — and that's key to having the best second half of life possible.

Health and vitality are critical elements in our attempts to design the second half of our lives, there are several proven strategies we can follow to increase our healthspan, or in other words — to live younger longer.

About The Author

It wasn't until he was transitioning into the second half of life that Joel Shuflin discovered that most everything his health-conscious, organic-gardening mother had tried to teach him was true. Today, Joel and his team of healthspan evangelists educate and coach people of all ages to live longer younger. Working in collaboration with the Shaklee Corporation, Joel and his team blend coaching, science, and common sense nutrition to help families find solutions that are in harmony with nature. He can be reached by email at joel@azlifeplan.com, or visit his website at azlifeplan.com

Notes

1. Sena, M. "Senior Care Industry Analysis 2018 — Cost & Trends." Fast Casual Industry Analysis 2018 — Cost & Trends. https://www.franchisehelp.com/industry-reports/senior-care-industry-analysis-2018-cost-trends/

2. US Census Bureau. "An Aging Nation." U.S. Trade with Haiti. April 10, 2017. https://www.census.gov/library/visualizations/2017/comm/cb17-ff08_older_americans.html

3. Guarino, Ben. "The Case for Cockroach Milk: The next Superfood?" The Washington Post. July 26, 2016. https://www.washingtonpost.com/news/morning-mix/wp/2016/07/26/the-case-for-cockroach-milk-its-the-most-caloric-protein-on-earth-scientists-say/

4. Reinberg, Steven. "It's Never Too Late to Get

Healthy." ABC News.
https://abcnews.go.com/Health/Healthday/story?i
d=4507742&page=1

5. Johns Hopkins Medicine. "It's Never too Late:
   Five Healthy Steps at Any Age."
   https://www.hopkinsmedicine.org/health/healthy_
   aging/healthy_body/its-never-too-late-five-
   healthy-steps-at-any-age

6. Wu, Ryan T.Y., and Wen-Hsing Cheng. "New
   Insight into Telomere Maintenance." *Aging* 2, no.
   5 (2010): 255-56. doi:10.18632/aging.100147.
   https://s3-us-west-
   1.amazonaws.com/paperchase-
   aging/pdf/glkl9qmrdxosqxpxv.pdf

7. Blackburn, Elizabeth H., Carol W. Greider, and
   Jack W. Szostak: The Nobel Prize in Physiology
   or Medicine 2009.
   http://nobelprize.org/nobel_prizes/medicine/laure
   ates/2009/press.html

8. Vivix. https://near-
   me.myshaklee.com/us/en/shop/healthysolutions/c
   ellularaging/product-_p_vivix_p_

9. Haley, C. B., "Cross-Sectional Analysis of
   Telomere Length in People 33-80 Years of Age:
   Effects of Dietary Supplementation,". Chiropractic
   Resource Organization,
   http://www.chiro.org/nutrition/ABSTRACTS/Cross
   -Sectional_Analysis_of_Telomere.shtml

10. The Center for Genetics, Nutrition and Health, "The importance of the ratio of omega-6/omega-3 essential fatty acids," October 2002, https://www.ncbi.nlm.nih.gov/pubmed/1244290 9/

11. Maxwell, John, *The John Maxwell Company*, July 12, 2016, http://www.johnmaxwell.com/blog/the-view-from-the-top-of-the-hill

12. Bramstedt, K. A. (2001). Scientific breakthroughs: cause or cure of the aging 'problem'. Gerontology, 47(1), 52-54. Retrieved 6 1, 2018, from https://www.karger.com/article/abstract/52770

The Volunteer Experience

By Holly McFarland

Beginnings

My personal story of volunteerism has come full circle as I approach my retirement years. My journey started at a young age when I, like many girls in the 1960s, worked as a candy striper at our local hospitals, delivering flowers to patients. As I grew up, the question was never, "Do I want to volunteer?" but was, "What kind of volunteering do I want to do?" It was an expectation of what we do as members of a family and community that care for one another. I have instilled this same value in my daughters, who are continuing this value of volunteerism in their lives and with their children.

My volunteer work has taken many directions throughout my life including political phone banks, dancing and singing with a performance group for local charities, Big Brothers and Sisters in my college years, Meals on Wheels with my children, and over eight years working with hospice. Each of these experiences has enriched my life with a satisfaction that is hard to measure.

As I have been writing this chapter, I too have been searching for that next meaningful opportunity. Having a passion for working with women, I have found an organization that could benefit from my career development experience and skills, helping underprivileged women with their career planning and job search. I am eager to start this new journey!

To prepare you to discover your own volunteer opportunities that fit your retirement objectives, and align with your best, true self, this chapter will help you explore the meaning, benefits, purpose and steps.

Meaning of Retirement and Volunteerism

Retirement means different things to different people and is an uncharted territory. Many of us look forward to retirement as a time when we can finally do all of the things we dreamed about but never had time to do because of work and/or raising a family. This could include things like traveling, starting new hobbies or bringing back old ones, reading, or volunteering. The list is endless. However, for some people this can be a difficult time of transition, especially for those who find the task of constructing a new life daunting.

When you were young, you may have been asked the question, "What do you want to be when you grow up?" This question looms large as one approaches retirement. Keep in mind that the average person will live about 25 years after retirement. That is a long time and most people would become quite bored without some meaningful activities. What exactly are your dreams? How can you make this next chapter in your life purposeful? How can you continue to grow? This is your opportunity to think about the things you have always wanted to do and to create a life that is fulfilling and rewarding.

Volunteer work is one of the most meaningful, rewarding, and formative experiences a person can have in his or her retirement years. It is also a vibrant component of our society. It can make an immeasurable difference in the lives of others by providing help to people in need, assisting with worthwhile causes, and helping to build strong communities. But the benefits can be even greater to the person doing the volunteering. This is an easy way to explore all your interests and passions.

While retirement is often portrayed in advertisements as a time to concentrate only on yourself, it is not how many people choose to live their later years. A survey of pre-retirees, when asked about their retirement aspirations, had varied visions. A majority (55%) said they wish to spend more time with friends and family and a third said they want to become involved in charity or volunteer work. According to the survey results, most retirees fulfilled their primary retirement aspiration.[1]

Benefits of Volunteering

Human beings see huge value in contributing beyond themselves when they retire. A study done at the University of Michigan revealed that persons who regularly volunteer their time heighten their overall zest for living and increase their life expectancy. Studies on the aging process have reached a similar conclusion. People who directly assist others, who share themselves openly, are healthier, happier, live longer, and lead more productive lives.[2]

We live in one of the most generous nations in the world. According to figures from the Organization of Economic Cooperation and Development, some 60% of Americans regularly engage in some kind of charitable activity, compared to an average of about 40% for other developed countries.

A study from Merrill Lynch and Age Wave found that Americans offered almost 8 billion hours volunteering for charitable causes, from church activities to political organizations to helping out neighbors and strangers. While Americans of all races and ages contribute their money and time, retirees are the ones who reach out the most.[3]

Volunteer: It's Good For You!

Volunteering is not only good for others, it's good for you.

Over the past two decades, we have seen a growing body of research that has established a strong relationship between volunteering and mental and physical well-being. With new studies being done, we are finding more and more benefits linked with volunteering, especially when volunteering after retirement.

The beneficial effects of volunteering on your physical well-being include:

- Lower mortality rates
- Less symptoms of chronic pain

- Reduced stress levels

- Fewer physical limitations

- Greater functional ability

- Increased strength and energy

- Lower disability

- Decreases risks of heart disease

- Less likely to develop high blood pressure

Research suggests that participation in volunteering activities can also have important mental well-being benefits that include:

- Decrease your risk of depression

- Increases self-confidence and self esteem

- Can bring fun and fulfillment to life

- Lowers the risk of dementia

- Helps counter the effects of stress, anger and anxiety

- Keeps the brain active, which contributes to a person's cognitive health

- Promotes happiness

According to Shawn Achor, author of *The Happiness Advantage*, who spent more than 10 years researching happiness and lecturing at Harvard University, "From a scientific standpoint, when we're happy and doing work we feel good about, the neurotransmitter dopamine is released in the brain. Dopamine improves our overall sense of well-being and increases our capacity to learn, be creative and experience increased levels of vibrancy."[4]

Volunteering can help you stay physically and mentally active. A study released by John Hopkins University in 2009 revealed that volunteers actually increased their brain functioning. Volunteer activities get you moving and thinking at the same time.[5]

Reignite Your Purpose

Aside from the physical and mental benefits, volunteering provides a whole host of opportunities for us to stay active and engaged with life. It offers us a chance to have new experiences, learn new skills, and expand our current skill sets. In addition, it can prove an effective way for you to re-establish a sense of identity as well as purpose in life.

Having a sense of purpose, a commitment to something outside of ourselves, is central to living a fulfilling, engaged life. Our increasing life expectancy — now 33 years greater than a century ago — offers us a novel opportunity to discover and embrace our purpose in the second half of life, to leave a meaningful legacy, and to connect with something great than ourselves.[6]

So what is purpose? Purpose can be grand — and important — and very broad where you can change the lives of hundreds of thousands of people, or it can be very personal and meaningful only to you.

Authors Sanjiv Chopra and Gina Vild, in the book *The Two Most Important Days*, state that you can find purpose in one of two ways:[7]

The first one is to reflect on it. It will come to you. Ask yourself what gives you the greatest joy. What do you really want to do with your time and talent? You might try this exercise that Chopra and Vild recommend:

- At the end of each day for a month, write down two or three things you did that day and give it a score from 1-10, where 1 means you were miserable, and 10 means it brought bliss. At the end of the 30 days, strike out all the ones that scored 1 to 5. Those that score 6-10 will resonate for you. Do more of those things and your purpose will come to you.

- Make a pie chart of what's important to you, such as work, family, and personal interests. Then make another pie chart of how you're spending your time. Do the two charts reflect each other? When you spend your time in ways that are really important to you, it will help direct you to your purpose.

The second way to find your purpose is to back into it, by tackling a cause that matters greatly to you. You may witness something horrific and you have the fortitude, the grit, and the compassion to say —

this is unacceptable, and I'm going to make a difference here. You have no idea when you start that it will become your life's purpose.

As Baby Boomers continue to retire, an increasing number of people will be looking for what comes next and seeking meaning in this new chapter of life. Many have never really considered their purpose up to now. Volunteerism is one way to meet this need. It not only provides us with the opportunity to get involved in a cause that we might be passionate about, but also provides the chance to look beyond our own circumstances and appreciate what others are experiencing.

Finding The 'Right Fit' Volunteer Experience

Read just about any book on career choice and you'll find a theme that runs through them all — choosing a career is all about finding the "right fit." The same is true for volunteer work. And it all starts with you.

Before you can tell your life what you want to do with it, you must listen to your life telling you who you are. Any search for a good fit starts with a good look inside yourself. This self-assessment begins by asking yourself three questions:

1. What do you like to do? Here, you might consider all the things that are really fun to you. Consider the ways you spend your time that make time fly, where you're so engaged in the doing that you don't have any thoughts of time.

2. What do you do best? Here, you might consider all of your strengths. Think about what you are naturally good at doing? Identify those top strengths that you would enjoy using in your volunteer work.

3. What are your priorities in retirement? Here, you will want to consider how important volunteer work is to you and how much of it, you want to do.

The more you know about yourself, the better you will be at finding that "right fit."

Steps In Finding And Landing That Perfect Volunteer Position

Let's look at the steps to take as you begin this journey. Hopefully these steps will help you gain clarity about the type of life and volunteer work you want to pursue.

Step 1: Begin By Identifying Your Goals In Retirement

Seek out your desires and have a purpose for your retirement. Volunteering is a wonderful way to enjoy a meaningful and fulfilling retirement.

Retirement is an opportunity to create a life that reflects more closely, who you are.

First, think about why you want to volunteer?

- What is it that you want to get out of it?

- Is there something specific you want to achieve?

Second, take time to think about what you would like to do. A powerful exercise to help you break through any barriers is to describe your "ideal day."

Instructions: Close your eyes and settle your mind. Imagine that you are writing a movie script depicting a day in your ideal retirement life. Describe every detail, your feelings, and your activities, as well as the people with whom you are interacting. Open your eyes.

What did you see during your "ideal day"? What surprised you? Now think about what activities or experiences you want to make time for.

Step 2: Research The Issues Or Causes Important To You

While you are considering your purpose, begin to research the issues or causes important to you. You'll broaden your options and you may find a cause that really speaks to you.

This is a time for testing and exploring.

- Focus on interests and causes you find compelling

- Make a list of organizations whose mission connects with ideas you are passionate about. Visit their websites

- Keep a notebook of your thoughts and ideas

- Put together a personal board of directors to get feedback from

Step 3: Identify Your Top Values And Motivators

This is a time for introspection and looking inside yourself.

Our values form the basis for our choices about what we will and will not do. They are those things that you find valuable or desirable. They can be assessed most easily by asking yourself the questions:

- What is important about doing that work?

- What are some possibilities?

People who achieve and have success at work express their values through their work. As you look at volunteer positions, be sure to consider how many of your top values will be met through the work? This is an important factor for finding fulfillment in the work.

It is equally as important to understand what motivates you, so that you can include those considerations in your volunteer work design as well.

Ask yourself:

- What motivates you to get up in the morning? Think of the last five days. On which of those days did you bound out of bed, ready to go? What was happening those days that made you eager to get going?

- What are your top motivators at work? What job duties, work missions and environments made you love your work?

- What is it that energizes you?

Looking at your answers to these questions, what are the most important work-related motivators to look for in your volunteer work?

To be motivated is to feel inspired and excited — to look forward to doing something. What motivates one person can be very different for another. Consider what motivates you and think about what you will need in your volunteer work that will feed your top motivators. Perhaps you are passionate about an organization's mission or you want to engage in community service while being involved in a hobby at the same time.

Some common motivators that have been expressed by others include:

- Challenging and interesting work

- Opportunity to be creative

- A chance to make a contribution

- A sense of achievement

- Recognition for our achievement

The bottom line is: It's your motivators and values that engage you or keep you engaged in your work.

Step 4: Determine Your Interests And Skills

To help determine what kind of volunteer job you might enjoy, explore your interests and skills. Often, doing what interests us keeps us motivated. Ask yourself if you miss the work you did before retirement and if there is something similar that you could do. Alternatively, would you like to do something new and different?

Acknowledge your skills and consider those you have to offer. Take an inventory of your skills and competencies. You can do this by making a list of positions you've held (both paid and unpaid activities and work). Draw a line down the center of a blank piece of paper. For each position, list what you "liked" on one side, and on the other side list "dislikes." Knowing what you want to avoid in your volunteer work is as valuable as knowing what you want to include. As you do this exercise, distinct skills and passions you have enjoyed over time will emerge.

Some other key items to think about:

- Consider your business skills and leadership roles acquired along the way

- Look at employing your skills and knowledge in new ways

- Identify the skills that you want to carry into this next chapter of life and determine how they could be applied to volunteer roles

- Perhaps you would like to learn a new skill or gain exposure to a new situation; consider seeking a volunteer position where you will learn something new

At this stage of life, we are "Masters," meaning we have competencies that we have developed and practiced over the years. A good fit as a volunteer is to find a way to put that mastery to the best use to serve your passions.

Step 5: Explore Opportunities That Align With Your Values, Motives, Interests And Skills

- Investigate each organization whose vision connects with your interests and values

- Attend meetings, fund raising events, and other activities of the organization

- Ask questions and meet with individuals who already have connections with the organization

- Try to visit organizations to get a feel for the culture

- Put your plan together including a volunteer resume

Now is the time to determine where you are going and to put a plan together.

A major mistake we make in this process, is that we look at our next job or volunteer work based upon what we have already done, instead of what we want to be doing. Instead, ask yourself, what will light you up, based upon your motivators and values? Then ask yourself, how do I use my experience, knowledge, and skills to leverage that?

Step 6: Write A Resume To Position Your Candidacy For The Volunteer Roles You Are Interested In

- Design your volunteer resume to introduce yourself and showcase your skills, talents, and experiences to the organization you'd like to volunteer with

According to expert resume writer, Samantha Nolan of Nolan Branding, writing a resume to position your candidacy for community-based volunteer roles will emulate the brand you created for career positions. You will, however, want to ensure your resume, and potentially your letter of intent, sends a clear message that this is your genuine target as you transition into a different phase of your life's journey.

To create a sound resume as a retiree seeking volunteer opportunities:

- Open with a "Qualification Summary" which focuses on your related experience from your professional and possibly your prior volunteer experiences.

- Next, present a "Selected Highlights" section where you will focus on your most relevant experience. In this section, include highlights from the experience you possess.

- Within your "Professional Experience" section, go back through about 10-20 years of your experience. This would mean omitting many of your earliest experiences.

- Partner your resume with a targeted letter of intent that provides for added transparency about your current stage in life.

It is never too late to get started. Whether you just retired or are in your later years there is an opportunity out there for you. For those who participate in volunteering, you'll find yourself gaining a sense of control, feeling appreciated, having a sense of purpose and being able to "give something back" — all important factors in your quality of life.

Tammy Lake, a retiree in Ohio who works for Habitat for Humanity, says volunteering keeps her mind sharp, and cites the most beneficial element of her volunteering as her belief "that I am making a difference."

Jim Williams, also a retiree in Ohio who works at a homeless shelter and a local hospital, feels he has enjoyed his retirement largely because "volunteering gave me another purpose in life. It lets me interact with folks my age and younger, bringing a new purpose in life every day, along with a new learning experience."

This rewarding experience has become a part of Tammy and Jim's new autobiography. Everyone loves a good story, so make yours the best it can possibly be.

About the Author

Holly McFarland is Director of Franklin University's Center for Career Development, Owner of HSM Consultants, and Retirement Coach with Lifelaunch Consulting. As a Retirement Coach, Holly helps pre-retirees define and design their next chapter in life with purpose and intention. She also serves on the board of the Retirement Coaches Association. Holly received her MBA from Franklin University and holds professional certifications in Retirement, Career, and Executive Coaching. Holly dedicates this chapter to her daughters, Amy and Meghan, who are a constant reminder that the happiest people are not those getting more, but those giving more. Contact her at Holly.Mcfarland5@gmail.com.

Notes

1. Jacob Schroeder, "Volunteering Makes You Happy in Retirement," *Advance Capital Management Financial Living Blog*, August 17, 2016, http://blog.acadviser.com/volunteering-makes-you-happy-in-retirement.

2. Richard Johnson, *What Color Is Your Retirement?* (St. Louis, MO: Retirement Options, 2006).

3. Tom Sightings, "7 Reasons to Volunteer in Retirement," *U.S. News & World Report*, November 16, 2015, https://money.usnews.com/money/blogs/on-retirement/2015/11/16/7-reasons-to-volunteer-in-retirement.

4. Shawn Achor, *The Happiness Advantage: The Seven Principles That Fuel Success and Performance at Work* (London: Virgin, 2011).

5. "Health Benefits of Volunteering," *AARP: Create the Good*, http://createthegood.org/articles/volunteeringhealth.

6. Natalie Eldridge, ed., *Live Smart after 50!: The Experts Guide to Life Planning for Uncertain Times* (Boston, MA: Life Planning Network, 2013), p. 142.

7. Sanjiv Chopra and Gina Vild, *The Two Most Important Days: How to Find Your Purpose and Live a Happier, Healthier Life* (Sydney, N.S.W.: Hachette Australia, 2018).

Starting A Business In Retirement: Think Before You Leap

By Donna Martin

It can hit like a lightning bolt or arrive slowly like *Invasion of the Body Snatchers* — starting a business in retirement. Whether you experienced a sudden inspiration, or the idea has seeped in over time, starting a business in retirement can be likened to a time past when we spotted a pretty girl or a handsome guy across a room.

From afar, we mentally assign him or her a myriad of attractive traits to go along with our first impression. Once we start to talk or even date, the reality can be much different than what we imagined. It's my hope that you think of this as business dating advice — consider it and make your best decision.

As a tenured business owner and coach, I feel compelled to give you a look at both sides of starting a business in retirement. My natural inclination is to cheer anyone who wants to roll the dice. Business can be invigorating, exciting, and an outlet for talents that few other pursuits provide.

With the opportunity to create something new and maybe even put a family name on it, to repurpose years of experience, or get the satisfaction of watching a concept turn into reality, the thought of starting a business can be seductive. The pride of putting "owner" on a business card and being the force behind an enterprise can be alluring.

Just two years ago, retirees were creating one quarter of all new businesses in the U.S., a number that continues to rise. They do it for a myriad of reasons. Here are a few I hear:

- They are energized thinking about making money in retirement by doing something they love.

- They are anxious to make up for time lost work, work, working to earn money when another pursuit would fulfill a lifelong dream.

- After years of toiling for others, they want to keep the rewards they create.

- They are motivated to prove to themselves (or their friends, their spouse, or their former business buddies) that they've got what it takes.

While all can be good reasons to take the leap into entrepreneurship, remember, looks can be deceiving. I forced myself to give equal time to the downside of business creation because I've seen people get second mortgages to finance businesses that never made a dime or waste precious time chasing a dream they realized early on they didn't want to catch.

Retirement alone creates a lot of angst. The level of anxiety created by voluntary retirement has been measured as equal to the stress of getting married. Forced retirement puts trauma levels off the charts.

Mixing retirement with a venture into the unchartered waters of a business startup could be more than an individual or couple can withstand.

Retirement time is ripe for differences to surface in couple relationships from who will do the everyday chores, whether to relocate, how much time to spend traveling or with the grandkids, how to spend money, etc.

When we consider that division of household duties ranks ahead of sex in causing marital arguments in retirement, what kind of ramifications can be expected when one spouse wants to start a business? It is risky. Without an adventurous spirit, it can seem terrifying, especially when the investment and time commitment are large. Proceed with caution.

Please note: You can skip ahead to "Five Reasons You Should Start A Business In Retirement" if you have the complete support of your venture by your significant other, money to lose without causing pain, lots of time to invest without regret, and no need to make a profit.

If you haven't turned the page yet, we'll start with a few of the most common deterrents.

Five Reasons You Don't Want To Start A Business When You Retire

Money

It's common to believe that there will be little investment, really. Starting with no plan to invest much in your business is naïve. If you must drive, you'll buy gas. What about supplies? No business cards, really?

Will your computer support your venture, or will you need new programs? Staff, even part time, is never free. Inventory? Client meetings? Marketing pieces? Bookkeeping? Social media? They all require cash (or credit). So, while the initial investments may be small, they will add up. Are you ready for that? Is your spouse ready?

When staff is required, the payroll is obvious, but many other expenses almost seem invisible. They get swept into shopping trips for family essentials and don't stand out as "business expenses."

Rarely do new business owners set up financial accounting out of the gate which means they can go months and even years not really knowing what the business is costing them. The gasoline bills and the cost of eating out can double easily. Often, the non-business-owner spouse is the one to detect the expense creep which causes questions and perhaps resentment.

Acknowledging that a new business will take capital, putting a number on the amount to invest and accounting for the expenses as they are incurred often is the last thing a business creator wants to do. It's tedious, not usually in their wheelhouse, and forces him or her to confront the fact that this pursuit won't be free.

Even the best of businesses doesn't turn a profit, sometimes for years. If generating revenue is a big motivator for starting a new venture, you may want to date a different girl or guy.

Time

Starting any business can be a very time-consuming adventure. It just is. Making your own schedule and taking vacations at will isn't really in the cards for most business owners. Most of the owners I've coached thought that freedom would be a given once they started their businesses.

Many found just the opposite. If they are in it alone and they don't show up, nobody shows up. Even with a dependable staff, it's taken them years to get even close to freedom. Would a business tie you down?

Freedom from a schedule is one of the biggest myths about being a business owner. In the best of companies, often the owner is a key component to success. Consulting, which is a common avenue for retirees going into business, usually is a one-man or one-woman show. Clients have needs and they take precedence over the consultant's schedule.

With employees, the owner's presence is even more crucial. The adage about the cat being away can be an issue. But even with the most dedicated people, direction and motivation are critical. If the owner is integral to the venture making money, when the owner is absent so is the revenue he or she would produce.

This may sound discouraging. It's better to consider it now than at the time you must explain why a long-planned vacation must be cancelled or why you're home less now than when you had a "real job."

The Plan

Yes, there should be a plan, and more than something written on the back of a napkin at breakfast with a buddy. What's the vision? Why are you doing it? How much will you invest and for how long? Who will buy your product or service and how will you find them? Will you need staff? This is just a start. Libraries and bookstores have great resources for building a rudimentary business plan.

The U.S. Small Business Association, www.sba.gov, has an abundance of free resources to assist people wanting to start a business, with everything from a step-by-step template for creating a business plan, to online training, and even local consulting through SCORE. SCORE is comprised of retired business owners and managers in your area who give free advice to budding small business owners. The Veterans Administration, https://www.va.gov/osdbu/entrepreneur/, has an equal number of resources and offers loans and grants for business startups.

Just as business creators can sometimes shun the planning process, some get stuck in it. They write the plan, rewrite the plan, edit the plan, etc. It's less risky than implementing the plan. I know a retiree who said he spent six months getting ready to go into business and spending startup money before he took the plunge. He panicked when saw his startup funds running out, so he started selling.

Keep in mind that the size of the plan should be commensurate with the size of the business being created and the amount of investment. Small investment equals small plan, etc. Creating a plan forces an examination of the critical elements of a business concept and can derail the idea before money gets spent. That is not a bad thing. If a forced examination of the nitty gritty is enough to squash enthusiasm, then that girl or guy isn't a good match. It's time to move on.

Don't skip the planning step. Lots of people do and live to regret it.

Your Job Description

Most new entrepreneurs want to do a lot of what they love — consulting, baking, fixing cars, painting, taking photographs, making furniture, or any of the number of other pursuits that inspire them. Then there are the things they don't like, aren't good at or both — like bookkeeping, hiring, supervising, keeping an up-to-date client database, writing blogs or Facebook posts, selling, and marketing. Fill in the blanks. Many of those tasks will need to be done. If he or she is a "solopreneur," only one person will get them done or not. (See the above section, Time.)

Of all the tasks needing attention, selling is the one most ignored by new entrepreneurs. It falls into the category of "not why they got into business."

Doing what inspires is a far cry from selling it. In addition, owners can become very attached to their output meaning when a prospect doesn't buy, it can be personally offensive. Not a good place to be.

As a result, selling can become an Achilles heel. Believe it or not, many entrepreneur wannabes believe the myth that, once people know they have a service or product to offer, demand will happen. What a surprise it can be when it doesn't. Emailing one's contacts normally does not create an order flow.

Selling normally requires personal contact, a robust marketing plan or both. It takes courage, tenacity, and the willingness to be told "no." The inability to sell can become a fatal business flaw.

Then there's bookkeeping. If a prospective owner won't keep track of expenses how will that work out? What about supervision? Managing people is one of the hardest tasks business owners must do. That's why many of them don't do it.

Is the prospective owner willing to do what he or she doesn't like to do?

What Is Required?

Business owners need a lot of discipline, patience, flexibility, and perseverance. Success in business does not happen quickly or with fanfare. It's slow (maybe nonexistent at first), and beset with backward slides. For those looking for immediate gratification, a new business venture is not a good date.

Owners who make it are adept at rolling with the punches, have a high tolerance for frustration, and accept that success in a new business cannot be gauged with the same ruler they measured success in a 20- or 30-year-long career. Agility to move with the current, pursue unexpected opportunities, fake it until you make it — these are other essentials for success as a new entrepreneur.

Understanding that business creation is a marathon and not a sprint is one key to making a good decision about whether to start a business or not. Years get more precious as we age. Considering how many years will be involved in a business undertaking is vital when making the decision.

After all that doom and gloom, here comes the bright side — the awesome reasons to start a business in retirement.

Five Reasons You Should Start
A Business in Retirement

We Aren't Old

The actuaries say men and women will live to their mid to late 80s. One in 10 of us will live to age 90, and one in five until 95. If 60-65 is retirement age, that leaves plenty of time to live another life. Our talents are ripe to be repurposed. Compared to newly minted business owners, tenured professionals bring the kind of depth and credibility only experience provides. We have energy and creativity in reserve.

Not only have you honed your primary skill, but learning to deal with people, making significant decisions, and creating new answers to old problems, are all skills that can be used out the gate as you start your business. What an advantage.

If Not Now, When?

Many retirees have dreamed their whole lives about piloting their own ships. Long years in corporate life often give rise to thoughts about all the ways a business would be better — if only they owned it. Retirement is the perfect time to ensure that when the curtain closes there are no regrets. With a good plan, a cap on investment, and passion for the pursuit, what do you have to lose? Of course, great disappointment and even some embarrassment could result. Weighed against the angst of thinking we should have done it but didn't have the courage or wouldn't take the time, which is worse? Why not follow that dream?

Time

We gain 40-60 free hours each week when we retire, plenty of time to undertake a venture that is time intensive. Truth be known, those hours can be hard to fill.

Taking a realistic look at what will replace the activity that dominated life can be sobering. It's easy to believe those empty hours will naturally fill up. For many people, they don't. Not so if you have a business. Entrepreneurs will tell you all day long that the list of things to do in your business is endless.

Money

Often, startup funds are readily available. Many retirees can devote part of their nest egg to a business, especially if they believe it will pay them back sooner or later. With their financial ducks in order, they can take a well-considered risk. Some already could be spending a considerable amount of money on a hobby that can be replaced by a business.

Sharpen The Saw

The mental stimulation of a challenge can be an elixir for longevity. Research confirms that, as we age, mental activity and attitude are as important to health as physical activity.

In addition, boredom and lack of social connection in the retiree population is contributing to depression, increased alcohol use and even suicide. What better way to prevent boredom and create natural social connections then by owning a business.

It's hard to beat the stimulation of creating something new, finding people that will buy it and striving for a profit. Business owners never will tell you they are bored. Tired, maybe, but not bored.

Is starting a business in retirement for everyone? Absolutely not. Is it for you? If the five reasons not to start a business didn't scare you and if you still have a burning desire to do it, you probably have met the right match.

About The Author

Donna Martin is a speaker and coach who focuses on entrepreneurs and people contemplating or in retirement. For 22 years, Donna owned and managed a multi-million-dollar business that she sold to a Fortune 500 company where she continued to work until her "retirement." Donna has been coaching and training since 2010. She holds an ACC through the International Coaching Federation and is certified by the John Maxwell Group, the Professional Business Coaching Alliance, the Retirement Project and Retirement Options. She combines her training, business experience, and her own attempts at retirement to bring authenticity and compassion to her practice. Learn more at: www.DonnaMartinInc.com

Potholes On The Road To Retirement

By Mary Blissard

People think of retirement as another notch on the timeline of life but it's more a fluid journey. A successful transition to a happy and fulfilling retirement begins and ends with your relationships, both inside and outside the home.

The good news is that you are the driver of your relationships — you set the tone, pick the path and meter the fuel that gives life to friendships, family roles, and social life. But as in any living thing with lots of moving parts, preparation and maintenance are required to make the way as smooth as possible.

'This Is Not What I Thought It Would Be': Two Opposing Visions Of Retirement

Communication is the shock absorber for your navigation on this unfamiliar road to your new life. As critical as good, clear and accurate communications are to your workplace relationships, they are even more important during and throughout the retirement transition.

For couples, a more obvious statement has never been said, but it is true for everyone particularly in expressing your visions, hopes and dreams of what you want retirement to be like. This is also vital in the specifics of the daily life, months and years ahead. Even a couple who can mind-meld, à la Star Trek, and barely need to speak a word to express how they're feeling or what they want, are surprised at the effort it takes to be heard in this new life chapter.

The sooner the real and essential communication begins before the actual retirement transition, the better shape a relationship can be in moving forward.

Some retirees, recognizing the differences in vision or difficulty in articulating their preferences will want to engage in counseling with a retirement coach or even a licensed marriage therapist. In this safe way, prior to the transition, the couple can start practicing inquiry advocacy and understanding of each other's positions.

Nothing can be better when a friend or partner says, "I hear you" or "I understand what you're saying" and this goes a long way towards goodwill over the route ahead, with its challenges and bumps.

What Time Is Dinner, Dear? Or, Our Lives Have Changed But I'm Still Doing The Housework!

Along the same lines as communication, the need to address how the roles each partner will assume/play may change in this new leg of life's journey. For boomers who were brought up in traditional households there may be a holdover expectation of what lies ahead, not only in household responsibilities but decisions about the direction a couple wants to go and who is going to "lead the way."

With the course change of retirement, roles and responsibilities of each partner will also adjust to the different pace and flow of these new days. All of a sudden the rationale of a regular household task, like vacuuming on Tuesday or mowing the lawn on Saturday, may be subject to comment or even criticism by the retiree, who is looking for improvements to make now with time at home.

More often than not the prospect of preparing dinner and doing the dishes, or being the sole maintainer of the cars or house is not the vision that a retiree aspires to, at least not indefinitely. And the feeling of being taken for granted can make some people want to "quit" the role they've played throughout their career years.

The shift to more equitable management of life and house chores is a phenomenon more boomers are willing to embrace in order to not just keep the peace, but to foster appreciation for each other's contribution as they navigate retirement.

In reality, the transition to retirement is the perfect moment to assess the roles each partner plays and make positive changes going forward.

Now That I'm Retired, People Expect Me To Drop Everything And Be There For Them!

Another obstacle to happy relationships that inhibits forward progress is competition for the retiree's time. For years, maybe even decades in one's work life, the use of time has been meted out to family and friends outside of work, if not necessarily subordinated to the demands on time a career required.

Some spouses or partners now expect that the newly found time in retirement be converted to time dedicated to their agendas, projects, and dreams. The honey-do list is not a myth, and even though it can be useful to get some progress on projects for the house or family, if it's not truly what a retiree desires, resentment and avoidance of the task or partner themselves will create more pressure on the relationship.

Even others outside your relationship may assume that since you are retired, you will have no reason not to come babysit your grandchildren, serve on the church board, or provide care for any elder relative who needs it. Particularly for women, the assumption by others that they need to fill their days with caregiving is quite common.

This is an ongoing phenomenon and those retirees who cannot articulate their time needs adequately will end up dejected, depressed or downright angry.

I Want To Make A Plan, But There Is No Commitment. The Loss Of Structure Of Your Days

Ask any retiree how they enjoyed the first weeks of their transition to retirement and you'll probably hear

- It was fantastic!

- I slept in every day!

- We have no agenda, no requirements to be anywhere and no tie required!

Sounds great, right? But the follow up answer sometimes only one month into retirement can go more like this

- I've finished my long-term to-do list, now what?

- It seems like it's Groundhog Day now the novelty has worn off.

- My partner loves the freedom but it feels like one big snow day to me.

- I need to get a life!

Putting some kind of structure into your retirement days has been proven to be beneficial and greatly increases the happiness level for boomers. Maybe it's because after many years in the workforce required a daily agenda, having a daily structure lends itself to the perception of control of your time.

This roadblock of no plan or direction for the use of your days can create havoc, especially if your partner is enjoying a thoughtful and planned life each day. A roadmap, even in the smallest version can alleviate the stress and uncertainty of what the future holds.

A retiree once said, "If I have to just play golf for the rest of my life, I will go crazy!" But it's not the golf that's the problem, it's the lack of purpose and meaning in retirement that causes the potentially hazardous detour.

If a retiree can figure out what is important and meaningful to them, and what they want to achieve in this new life era, the use of their time and daily structure will appear in an organic way. Volunteerism, education, travel goals, and new experiences, as well as social and family commitments, can be purposefully sought. But even if there are no specific goals you are pursuing, awakening each morning with an agenda in mind is the way to stay on track to contentedness, both personally and in your relationships.

Some folks have required that they are up, exercised and out the door by 10 o'clock each day. Others have a standing social commitment with friends or family once a week or month. Most retirees could benefit from regular volunteer activities that are meaningful to them, not just a filler in their calendar.

Daily structure lends itself to purpose, and purpose means movement. Movement is essentially the key to good emotional and physical health, something we all want to afford in the years ahead.

My Social Life Revolved Around Work, Now I See It Slipping Away. Loss Of Camaraderie And Connection

As the work life is winding down, colleagues and friends in the workplace become sentimental and nostalgic, promising continued outreach after the "honored one" departs. Retirees will tell you, it's just not true, and this is one of the detours they didn't see coming. For those who worked in an office environment or tightknit corporate structure, it's unimaginable that absence doesn't make the heart grow fonder. It really means, "out of sight, out of mind."

One benefit of connection with your work peers is that you are all on the same page of reference — no explanation is required when diving into conversation about people or events pertaining to work. And that familiarity and comfortability has taken time and mutually shared experiences to develop, and cannot be replace or duplicated overnight. It is especially evident in careers where camaraderie is not only encouraged, but highly valued, like the military or team-oriented professions. Additional benefits of the job were the relationships grown and fostered along the years. Unless there is a concerted effort by both the retiree and the colleagues, this bond and connection will necessarily weaken after retirement.

But what about the use of social media to keep or connect in this great big world? In this generation of boomers social media can be a tool to stay in touch, but the lack of actual presence of a friend or colleague can make this practice seem trite or not worth the effort.

With relocation, too, there is a disconnect from neighbors, friends, and social structures, like church groups, and golf/tennis/bridge buddies. Part of the grief experienced at the end of a career is the inevitable loss of connection and camaraderie that can be a devastating obstacle to the retiree's happiness in the next phase of life.

There are a couple of ways to anticipate the impact of separation from colleagues and friends. First, proactively seek and schedule opportunities to connect on a regular basis, even if it's only once a month or quarter.

This personal interaction, post-retirement, may emphasize your loss of connection more but it is a way to stay in touch in the manner you were used to.

Second, establish some social media outreach — a LinkedIn or Facebook page of your "excellent retirement adventure," or a group page for retirees and colleagues before you retire.

See if there is a willingness to acknowledge the loss of regular connection but also the importance to keep up contacts. An example of lament and regret is gathering at a colleague's funeral and wishing you had one last talk or visit to remember him or her by.

Finally, start adjusting to the idea of less frequent and intimate connection to occasional but more deep and meaningful encounters. This can be true for neighbors and friends, as well as for work relationships. It's not going to be the same when you retire but it can still be a functional and rewarding relationship.

My Time, My Way, My Retirement.
Keeping Sacred Boundaries

Although retirement has been around since the dawn of work, a theory persists that there is a "right way" to do it. Probably even more than when you first embarked on a career, and received unsolicited advice about how to choose your work, your home, and your partner, the impending retiree is now subject to other's ideas of what your retirement should look like.

Others' opinions on where you should live, what you should do with your time and even how you should spend your money can be offered in well-meaning ways but when it comes down to it, it's your retirement.

Examples of the perfect retirement life plan may be out there but realistically in order to be content and thrive, post-career, you have to find your own way forward. This isn't "Blind Man's Bluff" — arms outstretched and feeling in the dark for what you think will work — although trial and error are frequently used on a retirement path. And the uncertainty without a roadmap makes the retiree susceptible to other's opinions which might have no relevance whatsoever to your life. Two very important takeaways to remember on your retirement journey are to develop and have a plan for the road ahead, and to keep your boundaries sacred.

Retirement life planning is taking off with the increased longevity of boomers and the desire to make the most of the years ahead. Using a retirement coach can reveal choices, foster confidence and create a purposeful path that brings the retiree meaning and contentedness. Even in relationships, two paths may be in parallel but they most likely will not be the same for each person.

Acknowledging that and respecting an individual's vision, hopes, and dreams will allow a relationship room to breathe and thrive.

Those boundaries on your time, your choices, and your way of following the road to retirement happiness, will also create the space for you to find and keep joy in your relationships.

Proactively mapping out your retirement life journey will allow you to miss the potholes and arrive at your destination intact.

About The Author

Mary Blissard is an airline pilot and Certified Retirement Coach. She guides individuals, couples and pilots in finding their purpose and joy in the retirement transition and creating a path to achieve that vision in the life chapter ahead. Contact Mary at www.flyingforwardinretirement.com

Maximizing Technology For Ages 50-100

By Joe Grant

From the book *Origin*, by Dan Brown:

> *"Human beings are evolving into something different," he declared. "We are becoming a hybrid species — a fusion of biology and technology. The same tools that today live outside our bodies — smartphones, hearing aids, reading glasses, most pharmaceuticals — in 50 years will be incorporated into our bodies to such an extent that we will no longer be able to consider ourselves Homo Sapiens."*

What an interesting time we live in!

Unless you are overwhelmed by technology changing your life, you are likely under-informed. Whether you are over-informed or under-informed, you are a part of a dynamic society and likely to be affected by any significant changes.

Thus, technology by itself isn't the villain or the rescuer. It is change itself we resist, fear, or exploit to our benefit. So, as Johnny Depp said in *Pirates of the Caribbean*, "The problem isn't the problem. Your attitude towards the problem is the problem." Often, we just don't know what we don't know. We *do* know what we know, but we don't always know which part of what we know is outdated — nor do we know the consequences of not knowing.

How do we, then, find out what changes, including technology, are affecting us, and what can we select from ever-changing technology to help us cope with our lives as they now exist? *Our* lives! Our personal issues! And, why bother? Feel safer? Stay younger? Less angry, with more peace and calm? Clarity in these areas helps us select the path that is unique to you and yours. There is more control for you if you want a preferred future at any age, but the last third of your existence is an important time for you. Do you concur?

Let's seek a bit of clarity, then.

Our First Question Is: Know What?

By the time you finish reading this chapter you will be more outdated and behind the power curve then before. You will also be left behind in things that aren't important now. But we don't care about that category. Or do we?

The unimportant could be important tomorrow! Take AI, for example. If you don't know what AI is (artificial intelligence), you just proved my point. Do you know the difference between augmented reality and virtual reality? Did you ever put your head in an OCULUS GO and see the inside of a beating heart? "Who Cares?" you may ask.

We all want to be up to date on what's important to us personally. It is hard to know exactly what is (or should be) important when almost everything in the world is changing so rapidly, and often in disruptive ways. If you lived in a sand castle on the beach, the waves coming in every day mess around with your structure. Each day, they are bigger and also more frequent than the day before. Keeping your sand castle looking good requires a lot more attention than a few years ago, and maybe with more anxiety about the outcome.

Alvin Toffler predicted all of this in a book called *Future Shock*. Published in 1970, it essentially outlined what was observable even then — too much incoming change in too many areas. Society as we know it would never be the same. That was 50 years ago.

Here is your one-sentence, 50-year summary of the book and, as a small bonus, a summary of *The Third Wave* and *Powershift* (his second and third books about change): As the rate of change accelerates and the amount of change does the same over time, it will outstrip our human ability to adapt to it.

Adaptation is much easier if change is constant. There is more learning time, and less learning in multiple areas to stay current. "Just-in-case" learning used to be normal and could be relied upon for a longer period of time.

For example, a 4-year degree in a fast-changing field would be OK at graduation. You could count on getting a job with it and it was cost effective. Tuition relative to income was reasonable.

But as the rate of change increases we get imbalances, and in many areas. A 4-year degree leading to oil exploration jobs may now be obsolete in its curriculum by graduation. Additional education in any field becomes the norm to even stay relevant. The amount and nature of additional education required likely will grow, and also the cost to get it updated. "Just-in-time" learning becomes more the norm. "Google it," replaces a 4-year degree! Not really, but you get the idea!

You may have experienced and have noted even bigger and better examples of these effects. But, in any case, you are standing on a ledge looking way back down the mountain of change! Think about the 50 years since the book *Future Shock* was published. It is 1970, and:

- The 1968 Democratic Convention in Chicago is barely 24 months in the past.

- The Moon Landing has just happened. (The computer power used to navigate 240,000 miles through space is miniscule compared to the phone you now casually carry around.)

- In 1968, much of the United States still uses rotary telephones and the U.S. Postal Service to communicate. (There are no touch-tone phones or fax machines).

Two major technological events happened comparatively shortly thereafter:

- IBM Personal Computers appeared on people's desks (and Apple gets a first bite). Think about 1978 to now. Moore's Law predicted that computer power doubles every 2-3 years.

- The internet came alive out of UseNET — say, about 1980 to 1985. Shortly thereafter, computers everywhere in the world are able to "talk" to each other.

Fax machines came and mostly went. They are not a dodo yet, but almost. Next, the iPhone came to us in 2007, and now the computer in your hand makes phone calls, internet searches, and takes dictation (with speech recognition). Siri (though not a great conversationalist) may soon be smart enough to be my personal butler and deliver my breakfast via a drone from Starbucks.

Are you getting bored reading the above? If you are, you may be at risk of being a boring person! This is overwhelming and mostly unpredictable change, except that we can predict change is overtaking our capacity to cope with it. Congress cannot organize a 2-car funeral. And forget multitasking — the latest brain studies prove it is a myth. Look it up with your phone if you don't believe me!

Consider this: You could go now to Amazon.com and buy a copy of the book *Future Shock* — and perhaps have it shipped to you with a drone — but you also could just download it to your Kindle app in perhaps 20 seconds and read it on your phone.

Is this comforting to you? Is it disruptive to book publishers in any way?

You can call Uber or Lyft to drive you — or you could drive for them. But perhaps self-driving cars will replace drivers altogether. In 2017, London outlawed Uber because every cabbie in the city has to train themselves to have the entire city map memorized. And they need to work! How would you feel if your current job was replaced overnight by a chip? Is this gentle change or disruptive? Or both?

Your phone now knows who you are by recognizing your face, and cameras that identify you accurately are increasingly present so you really can't go anywhere without being recognized — unless you live in a very remote area and don't leave it. You could become Big Foot and live totally off the grid!

What part of this technology wave is disrupting to you and what is not? What is helpful? In a recent California State University brain study class for seniors (ages 55-93), I asked, "What part of technology do you like and what do you dislike?"

There were many comments as you might imagine, but the most memorable one from a 65-year-old, well-dressed and charming grandma went like this: "I don't like technology at all," she said.

I said, respectfully, "Well I'm sure you have some good reasons for feeling that way — would you mind sharing with the class?"

Her comment, after just a moment of hesitation: "Alexa Farts!"

Our next Question: So What?

This question implies that we can safely ignore the parts of tech that inconvenience us as individuals. Here are some quotations from the "Ostrich Operating System":

- "I really don't need to know that. I can learn it (just in time) from Google"

- "I'm safe with in my job, my tribe, my area, my whatever. The tech wave is destroying someone else's sand castle a few feet down the beach without hurting me at all! I'm immune to change right where I am!" (See London cab drivers, above).

- "Everything that can be invented has been already." (U.S. Patent Office from about 1880.)

The "So What?" question is only answered in terms of, "*Me! Me! Me!* How am I threatened?"

We live in what may be called a tribal society where there is less trust of the tribes over the hill. Our perceptions of change are very personal here, so let's have a look, briefly, at Abraham Maslow and his pyramid of personal needs (check Wikipedia for a quick review). Basically, you have to go up without skipping. Safety has to be satisfied before you roam up into Love-Belonging.

From Top to Bottom:

- Self-Actualization (the highest point)

- Esteem

- Love-Belonging

- Safety

- Physiological (the lowest level)

If we don't know what the layers are versus where we are on the pyramid, we are often going to make inappropriate choices. Choices are based on our perceptions of our environment and values; our perceptions of wants or needs in body, mind, and spirit come out of our brains, not just our senses.

For example, your nose is sensitive to pollen and suppose that pollen granules cause some irritating neural synapse to hit the area of the brain which then remembers that it should tell your "sneeze" muscles to do just that! All of this is done without much frontal cortex (conscious) thought. Thus, we decide to do something unconsciously before we consciously decide to do it.

The same sequence is present more than we would like to admit. Covering your mouth and nose may happen simultaneously as you realize that you are close to someone in an airplane or theater.

The most recent brain studies reveal some very interesting and a little scary observations showing how our brains are adapting to the onslaught of change, and often decide things milliseconds before our "conscious" mind is aware of it.

This is a big and unsettling discovery. Where you are on the pyramid is very influential in all choices, including those you make about technology. But who is making those choices *before* you act? Is someone riding shotgun with you while you look at a 4K TV in the electronics store? Why did you just buy a huge jar of pickles at Costco? It was a bargain to be sure, but who told you to do that? Was it self-esteem you are seeking? Or was it survival? I think not, but you are the only one who knows!

Where are you now on the pyramid? If you are very anxious and fearful, you will have a hard time moving on and *up* to self-actualization! What kind of tech could make you less anxious and fearful, or more healthy?

Perhaps an app called "Calm" could do wonders. What is *your* marginal gain from a heart pacemaker? It may offer a new life, but then you ask, "Will Medicare pay for it?" Has life become "low-hanging fruit?" Can a new heart valve give you 10 years or 20 years more? Choices all have value sets behind them, fueled by perceptions. Adapting to change will always require fulfillment of needs and wants.

Is the human brain evolving fast enough? Is yours? Why are we concerned about AI? And, again, we must get up close and personal about *you*? Who cares about the Star Trek costume neighbor, the new Muslim at Rotary, or Christians driving Uber because they fled Syria? Or Sikh neighbors (tribe) when your food supply or other bio needs are threatened?

A lecture on neuroplasticity in class today may or may not help you tomorrow. We tend to favor just-in-time ("Google it") learning and ignore just-in-case learning. Just-in-case learning, however, requires the merger of long- and short-term memory circuits. Could an app help with that?

And what about emergencies? Have we practiced fire drills at the office? How do we get out of this hotel if needed? What is the present situation? Who may need CPR in the class we just enrolled in? Again, these kinds of situations depend on merging short-term memory with long-term memory (think *MacGyver* on TV). Put *this* together with *that* and we save our life! Can we depend on AI to do that? Would you? Some AR (augmented reality) is being developed that helps.

There is another organization of value systems that you may relate to and use. You can look at your brain as driven by purpose and you can make tech choices consistent with purpose. Here is a little formula you may find helpful:

P-K-A-S-H-V

- Purpose

- Knowledge

- Attitude

- Skills

- Habits

- Vision

I see this sequencing as the elements of creativity and expression — you usually have to go through this sequence to get what you want or need, so it may help you find the technology you need to cope with changes you are experiencing within the above sequencing.

How can technology help you find purpose, select knowledge, enhance attitude, practice skills, and form habits to allow follow through and move towards your vision? Where are you on Maslow's mountain and what is your vision? Is it buying a new home soon? Or, do you need all-new LED lighting? Or should you simplify?

I sit in the dark sometimes and listen to a meditation on my iPhone, remembering from youth how a kerosene lamp looked in a dark room when lit — quite beautiful and warm. But, I don't need the iPhone to do it, or do I? Shall I do Sudoku on it to keep my brain nimble, or is a paper version even more effective?

Your answers must be right for your situation and environment. Thus a good retirement coach will be very curious to know your environment *and* suggest sources to modify it to help you, including types of technology, with *you* being in control of the selections!

Consumer choice is often impulse only and often wrong because we confuse wants with needs — the urgent vs the important, and so on. Technology in the form of products is especially relevant here. For example, when should you replace your iPhone? Or should I buy a Samsung G-7 phone? Or some other brand? Or just a flip phone for my Mom? Do I consider needs or wants? Habit enhancements like journaling? Reminders for Mom to take her pills?

A third way to look at yourself and changes in your life is to look at your life as a coin rolling along life's path, in almost perfect balance. If it is in perfect balance you should be moving forward blissfully at the pinnacle of Maslow's structure — his penthouse of self-actualization — living in one beautiful present moment of mindfulness after another!

Now, let's examine the coin. On one face are the internal arenas of body, mind, and spirit. On the other side are external arenas like work, family, leisure, health, finances, and personal development groups.

As long as all is in reasonable balance, the coin moves along through life's present moments with a minimal wobble. But let something happen that is destabilizing, and we humans all move rather quickly to first assess the degree of "wobble." If it is serious, we are right back down living in Maslow's basement apartment.

So, what technology helps you keep your life in balance? My wife just corrected some wobbles with a pacemaker that reports heartbeat data wirelessly from her bedroom. She physically feels 10 years younger, now.

A harder decision is whether to buy a new Apple Watch 3. Its health sensors are much more advanced now than a year ago, but what is the marginal gain in the arenas mentioned above? Reduced stress? Would her coin roll along better and why? Those of you who have health sensors, send us some advice. I would deeply appreciate it!

And, Finally, Now What?

Conclusion: Some suggest you first program your brain around the two sides of the coin to keep your balance within the six arenas. The body-mind-spirit connection has often been cited as the first step in finding internal balance — your reality as you record what you see smell, hear, taste, observe, process, and so forth, that creates *your* existence. As the coin rolls along we could assume one revolution per day where you keep a journal. Would it help you to have an electronic reminder to journal in writing each day? Supplemented by pictures?

If you post to Facebook, are you not already journaling? Except it is very public! How about an internal journal aid for just *your* private thoughts!? And technology must be dealt with on your terms. You are the programmer in this case.

Select the tech that avoids the wreck, then consider biological needs, safety, and self-actualization. You have goals in each of the arenas. Where does tech help with your balance in life? With regard to the value structures above, here are some more questions for you to ponder: What's your perception

302

of the amount of time you have? Is life too slow, so you are bored? Or is life too fast for you to appreciate? How about some low tech?

Watercolor painting might be a lot better for you now! Later, you could supplement your watercolor skills by downloading a painting course from the Great Courses. Or you could use an iPen! If an app gives you a big marginal gain at reasonable cost — even free — how will it help you in the six arenas or in the internal perception arenas of body, mind, and spirit?

One of the best brain apps currently available is Luminosity. There is a meditation app called Headspace. Yet, you can become calm by sitting on a bench in the Muir Woods — or any deep woods or quiet place. Does the app help you focus and follow through, or manage money?

For example, if it measures something like steps, calories, or money, it may be a start to improve your outlook. If you can measure something you can likely improve its value. Does it motivate you to have a better attitude, practice skills, or form habits? Does it bring you closer to others, but not too close? You decide.

But even limited outreach to others is a big sign of brain health in recent studies! Does your app aid memory and or other neural processes, or does it cause them to shrink? Einstein didn't know his own phone number! Did he need to?

Does any technology choice help you and others allow for growth? An app called Cozi can unite family or support groups because it ends confusion and separate scheduling. OmniFocus is a task management app people like, but you have to pay for it. Does it leverage other goals?

Note: Go for leverage not multitasking. Multitasking is a myth. For example, if a journaling app (try DayOne) can help with daily reflection and recording good results, you are really leveraging. Doing three things simultaneously is not good for you, but stressful. A Blue Zones subscription could help with multiple health goals and fitness at the same time. Longevity by itself is a poor goal but longevity paired with health and vigor is leverage.

Finally, does your action plan help keep you stable with P-K-A-S-H-V as your coin rolls along each day? With less stress, more joy, and more confidence in your present moments? Does it help you serve yourself and others in a fair ethical manner? Does it make aging a gift? Goals are for adults as rules are for kids. Does it help you set goals or keep them?

Final Thoughts About Change And, Particularly, Choosing Relevant Tech

According to Croft and Bolton, "Our heads are required to stay on a swivel these days, scanning for opportunity and information, fighting to maintain even the slenderest edge and advantage, desperate for relevance."

We all need a Weeble-like dynamic where we return to upright as opposed to the silly bobblehead, searching mindlessly for something relevant. *You are your own "true North"* — your best compass or intuitive Weeble that self-corrects. If tech enhances this sense of self, it is likely well worth it.

I hope this gives you some fair, effective, and ethical assistance the next time you bump into technology as a force of change, and that it gives you peace and calm to cope with this speedy life we all are living. Slow down! Rest! Technology that helps us smell the flowers and have warm relationships cannot be bad. But, good or bad, tech is not going away. And, eventually, Alexa will be taught some manners!

About The Author

Joe Grant is a former Financial Planner who, having helped people figure out how to save money, realized at some point that the next big task in life was to know what to do with it and help others know their best selves. Along the way, it was a mainly a lot of fun. There were, as in all lives, a few dark times, yet the bridge *back* to joy was worth building. Joe Grant, MBA, is a Managing Partner of Vantage Points, LLC, 2880 Sunrise Blvd, Suite 200, Rancho Cordova, CA 95742, Phone: 916-597-2649. Visit https://yourvantagepoints.com

Caregiving For A Spouse In Retirement

By Leslie Koc

It isn't often, but when I do see a triple-decker sandwich on a menu I don't think of how I'm going to eat that massive meal. I think about caregiving and all of the possibilities of how people in retirement can be challenged to care for others who are family members, friends or neighbors.

The term, "sandwich generation" was coined by Dorothy Miller in 1981 to describe women in their 30s and 40s who were sandwiched between caring for their children and their aging parents. With the increased life expectancy, the economic volatility of the job market, and its related financial challenges, in the 1990s, U.S. journalist Carol Abaya introduced another layer to the sandwich with the term "club sandwich generation" — adding the caregiving responsibility of grandchildren.

As a retirement coach, I observe the addition of yet another layer of caregiving responsibility for those in retirement. That "triple-decker sandwich generation" includes the caregiving of a spouse or life partner.

In most of the financial and nonfinancial retirement planning that occurs, the reality of caregiving for a spouse doesn't usually get the space and thoughtful planning it deserves. It isn't part of the picture of the happy couple touring their bucket list vacation or skimming the surface of the water in a brand-new boat.

The reality of one half of a couple needing care sometime in retirement seems logical, but accepting and planning for that escapes most of us until it happens.

My guess is that it's similar to buying a home in a hurricane-prone area. It's a beautiful home and yet there's this possibility that a hurricane may hit during one of the seasons while living there.

You don't want to live in the house with the windows boarded up all the time, but wouldn't you want to know about boarding up windows, how much it will cost to purchase the boards, and generally what you'd do if the hurricane forecast became a reality?

A friend recently asked me when I realized that I was a caregiver for my husband. I was crystal clear in my answer. It wasn't when we sat in our doctor's office and heard that my husband had mild cognitive impairment, the potential early stage of dementia.

It was when my husband announced soon after that he thought it best to give up driving. He was concerned that he might injure himself or someone else with a bad decision while behind the wheel.

At that moment, I realized that our lives would be changed forever and at that moment his progressive disease took a back seat to my immediate thoughts about how we would manage our daily lives.

Backtracking, what is caregiving? It's the help and assistance provided that someone needs with some or all of their activities of daily living.

Beyond help with personal care, it also includes emotional and advocate support. Being a caregiver can come about as a result of impairments related to aging, a disease, physical disability, or mental disorder.

When a spouse becomes a caregiver for their partner, the very definition of roles is thrown into the air and reassembled as the roles fall into new places. It's different for every couple, but that's not to say there aren't many commonalities that we can learn from each other.

One of the most central changes with one spouse becoming a caregiver is the loss of the support system that each person has most likely come to rely upon from the other spouse. It's that additional opinion, the yin and the yang of keeping things in balance, the one who holds the ladder or climbs the ladder, and the rest of telling a favorite joke. It changes suddenly or over time, but nonetheless, it's no longer the same.

In the realm of retirement planning, it's the sobering piece of what-if contingencies that financial planners suggest clients consider as they map out their future. As important as the financial stress of caregiving and illness is in planning a retirement portfolio and a budget, the emotional and physical toll it can take on a couple is one that dwarfs most everything else. If you're the one who is now the caregiver, recognizing that role is the first big step to creating a new normal life and finding happiness in it.

There are five major areas where caregivers can gain back control in their lives at a time when the ground may feel soft and moving from what you thought to be terra firma.

Self-Care

You may have heard the flight attendants' instructions at the beginning of any flight: In an emergency, when the oxygen masks drop down, place the mask on yourself before helping a child or other companion. In order to help others, you need to be in a capable position yourself. In the role of caregiver, maintaining your own health is a tall order despite the thought, "Of course I'll take care of myself".

When there's no one taking care of you or delivering a tender reminder, it's an easy slide to postpone preventative health appointments. Most things can wait unless and until they become a health crisis that can't be delayed. Then, like the tiny water drip that becomes a flooded floor, it can't wait and has greater consequences to taking care of it earlier.

Sleep, mindful eating, and exercise is the mantra for a healthy life, but how do you accomplish them when there are only 24 hours in a day and someone else is depending on you? The answer is "with intention." Planning for a healthy day creates a better possibility for that to happen than leaving it to chance.

A recent reminder from the National Sleep Foundation (NSF) notes that periods of sleep "restore and rejuvenate, grow muscle, repair tissue, and synthesize hormones."

Caregiving requires clear and creative thinking to stay ahead of new and changing situations. Exhaustion or fatigue affects a caregiver's mood and resilience. The NSF's current recommendation for those over 60 is 7-9 hours of sleep, allowing for individual needs. If you're not sleeping the minimum number of recommended hours, you and your spouse are limiting your ability to cope with daily challenges.

We're fortunate to live in an age of amazing access to good food. If preparing a meal together isn't possible, many alternatives are available in grocery stores or delivered to your door.

My husband and I created a master list of meals that we enjoy. It helps me when I'm feeling like I can't be any more creative that day with anything. I'm spent. The list is sorted in order of easy to time-consuming, but delicious.

For the last part of the mantra, exercise, take the long way anywhere. Since walking is one of the best forms of exercise, it's something that can be built into your day. Being outdoors has a bonus of adding fresh air and on days that outdoors isn't possible, open a window or the door and take a deep breath.

There's nothing quite like fresh air to clear the mind and the mood.

Stress is a normal part of life. In fact, a moderate amount of stress is okay because it keeps us focused and on task. The problem arises when the stresses of caregiving reach a limit where you can't get back to a refreshed state. It's a continual stress state that negatively affects our health and our ability to be of help to our spouse.

There are many techniques to help relieve stress including exercise, meditation, dance, and laughter. Two websites that focus on caregiver stress are www.aarp.org/caregiving and www.mayoclinic.org/healthy-lifestyle/stress-management.

Caregiver Versus Care Manager

What a difference a word makes. Giving care creates a picture of being the sole provider of the care a loved one needs. Managing the care for a loved one opens up the possibility and maybe even the permission to bring others into the picture as part of a care team. Why not give others the opportunity to show how much they care and want to help?

We live in a culture that favors a show of independence and strength. Asking for help is counter to an image we want for ourselves. But, in fact, we enjoy being able to help others. It's a head scratcher why we can't make the leap when the shoe is on the other foot. You don't know how others can help? Here's an assignment. Take the time to make a list in advance of what others can do. Have it handy when concerned people ask what they can do to help. Split it into categories:

- One-time tasks: The ones that anyone can do. Examples would be picking something up at the grocery store, raking leaves, or vacuuming a carpet. It may be small in the grand scheme of a day, but it's one less thing on an undone to-do list.

- Companionship: Sometimes, people don't know that just keeping someone company for a short visit can add a positive lift to a day for everyone. Add notes on what simple joys in a visit can include.

- Sharing the load: What are the responsibilities that you now have that would be easier if there was someone at your side? I can remember struggling with moving a table by myself. It got done, but with more grunts than maybe necessary.

- Food: Now, there's a huge opportunity. Many days can be a bit brighter when food is added. Whether it's someone preparing a meal for you, coming over to enjoy food together, or bringing a cup of coffee, it's all welcome. The ideas can be tailored to what brings you and your loved one pleasure.

- The heavy lifting. There's no doubt that caregiving includes responsibilities that are not easy, pleasant, or going to go away. You might be surprised to have a friend or family member who is up for the challenge, and without asking you'll never know.

Care Recipient

Reversing seats, how would you want to be included in your own daily activities and decisions? That question slows the tendency to take over the care recipient's life. Caregiving responsibilities gain momentum slowly and steadily, and some of it may be accelerated inadvertently by the caregiver.

It could seem easier to just do it rather than to take the time to allow the care recipient to try their best at self-care — and that's the double edge. It can get the job done, but it adds to the caregiver's load and diminishes the other person's degree of independence. The gift of patience is discussed later in this chapter.

Care recipients I've spoken with often relate stories of becoming invisible in the presence of their caregiver. Questions and conversations are directed to the caregiver rather than to them. Caregivers can help maintain the independence of their spouse with a redirection to them such as, "How would you like to answer that?"

Everyone has a life story to tell. It could be a slice of life or the whole enchilada. In either case, capturing a care recipient's story is an opportunity to bear witness to their life when they may not be able to do it themselves. There are lots of ways to get started.

An interview format is the simplest. With a list of open-ended questions — the ones that don't have simply yes-or-no answers — begin a conversation. Depending on whether, as a couple, you decide to record the responses for other family members and friends, you have choices of using the pencil-and-paper method, video or audio recording, or just appreciating the responses in the moment. Laughter, tears, and the warmth of reminiscing are sure to follow.

Big Picture

As a caregiver myself, I know I get caught up in the trees and forget to step back periodically to see the forest. I didn't seek this role in my retirement years, but I know that this is part of my retirement chapter. The strength I gain in embracing my caregiver role is that I can define it or at the very least, influence it.

Goals are just as important now as they were when my husband and I were planning our retirement. The value of setting daily and longer-term goals has a benefit for both the caregiver and the care recipient. It could be as simple as both of you being dressed by noon. When it happens, that's something to feel accomplished about and becomes a time to celebrate.

Without benchmarks of goals, daily life becomes a stream of one day to the next. Looking beyond today, having bigger goals creates a need for a plan. They're the ones you want to be able to look back upon 6 months or a year later and see progress to a positive outcome. I'm not suggesting a long-term goal of reversing an incurable disease, but I am suggesting goals that will make your and your spouse's life different and hopefully better.

Each person and each couple are in a unique place, and what improves life for one person is unlike what it is for another person. The conversation may bring about an initial sadness for things not going as planned, but taking a fresh look at what is now possible can be just as exciting and fulfilling as original plans. The operative word to use is "different."

It's a natural curiosity and need to want to understand more about a spouse's illness. The internet makes that possible in a big way. Not only can you learn, but you can get involved in organizations who are working to find a cure, advocate for services and programs, raise money to fund these organizations, and meet others who are similarly impacted. Influencing change, big or small, is empowering. It provides a sense of recapturing control in what otherwise feels like an out of control life situation.

Gifts

There are gifts that caregiving brings to my life. At the top on my list is that I've gained a daily perspective on what's really important and what is a minor issue. There's little time for the unimportant. It has given me permission to forgive myself for not living up to my standard of perfection.

An aphorism my husband would often quote to me, "perfection is the enemy of good" (attributed to Voltaire), is a frequent source of a smile. Most recently it occurred when I let the glimpse of a sheet corner show below our comforter as we finished making the bed together in the morning. At an earlier time, it would have caught my eye each time I passed the bed. Today it is more than good enough.

Examples of the gift of caregiver patience pop up at the most unexpected times. "Rushing" and "last minute" are terms of the past. Building in more time for what might be a simple task allows time to notice. It could be the color of the sky on a slow walk, the sound of water running in the shower, or the taste of a cooled cup of coffee. These moments would otherwise be lost in the blur of hurrying to get things done.

Although the topic of support groups can fit within the Self-Care area, it's here in Gifts because it goes beyond what's in it for you. Joining and participating in a support group creates new relationships with strangers with whom you instantly have a deep connection. Not only are you receiving the gift of a safe and welcoming place to share your challenges, but it's also a place where you can share what you know, have learned, and have tried. Support groups are in-person groups, online groups, for caregivers in general, and for caregivers of care recipients with a specific illness or disease.

Realizing that caregiving is making a positive difference in the life of another person can be a true gift beyond measure. In a life partnership or marriage, we do and are there for each other. Adding the role of caregiving takes it to a deeper level of human connection. It's giving, sharing, and (yes, at times) sacrificing for another.

There are plenty of days when the role of a caregiver is exhausting and unsung, and other days when caregiving is rewarding and loving. What's consistent throughout is the act of providing what a spouse cannot do for themselves.

Two of the descriptors that most often distinguish retirement from other life chapters are "freedom" and "flexibility." On the surface, they can be at odds with the life of a couple in a caregiver-and-care-recipient relationship. To recapture or include freedom and flexibility, it does involve coming to terms with a new picture of retirement.

It may not look like the original plan, but what time in life looks like the original plan? Keep in mind the five outlined areas of caregiving to assist you and your spouse in creating a new and different retirement chapter.

About The Author

Leslie Koc is a Certified Retirement Coach who supports clients in their quest to fully live their retirement years and to leave a legacy. After thirty-five years in corporate executive leadership and senior team development, Leslie designed her own retirement life chapter in Central Oregon where she teaches classes on the subject and coaches clients throughout the country in individual and group settings. Through a guided process, Leslie's clients have the opportunity to develop their unique retirement path and to make it a reality. For Leslie, retirement coaching isn't simply a vocation, it's a passion. Learn more at: https://www.linkedin.com/in/lesliekoc

Not If But When: Bouncing Back From The Lows In Retirement

By Laura Riddle

This book is a compilation of material, co-authored by a variety of experts. We wanted to cover many different aspects of the Retirement experience. Some got fun chapters and I got an important but not as fun one. So please read and don't skip this!

As a Licensed Marriage and Family Therapist and Certified Retirement Coach with over 40 years of experience, I address some really challenging issues and concerns, and provide useful, timely information and resources (I hope, without being a bummer).

Also, I have attempted to infuse some humor, none of which is intended to make light of serious subjects or real-life problems. To quote the singer, songwriter and fellow Baby Boomer Jimmy Buffet, "If we couldn't laugh we would all go insane."

Acknowledging and discussing uncertainty, fears and the inevitable low points and losses that come with Ageing, is often not an easy process. It's a lot more exciting and fun to focus on the positive and many likely "high" points and experiences.

However, it is helpful to look at all aspects of life in Retirement because with planning, hope and a balanced perspective, we can develop, and/or enhance the skills, strategies and attitudes that create the resiliency necessary to manage challenges and "bounce back" from adversity. Looking forward to this "encore" phase of life with optimism and enthusiasm is of course important. It encourages us to mindfully create the Retirement we want and so richly deserve.

By doing this, we can continue to grow into our best selves yet to come, experience the things we want to do, explore the places we want to go and spend time with people we love or even meet new ones with which to have new connections and adventures.

Hopefully we can and will have more fun, freedom and flexibility to be physically and emotionally healthy, socially and relationally connected. Thereby allowing us to engage in purposeful, meaningful activities and overall be less stressed and more fulfilled and happier.

Realistically we inevitably will encounter fewer positive situations but sticking ours heads in the sand pretending that we won't doesn't prevent them from happening. It usually just limits our options, as we haven't contemplated potential plan(s) of action to best manage the situations.

Plan and Act Before You Have To

My Grandmother lived to be 103 and I learned something important interacting with her all those many years. I learned to recognize impending transitions and to act before I "had to" because the situation had become a crisis. Sometimes we don't have that choice as unexpected events can and do happen. However, there are predictable changes that will occur in our lives, like it or not. We will likely experience a decline in some of our capacities and need to adjust to hopefully "age gracefully." Or I guess we can go kicking and screaming.

This is not to say that we must dwell and ruminate on the potential negative parts of getting older. Rather do our best to embrace, or at least acknowledge, discuss, and plan for likely challenges and changes. We can identify what might get in the way of living the life we want in retirement; be it financial, physical, emotional, social or even spiritual in nature.

Some people say that to ask such questions and anticipate possible barriers is being negative or looking for trouble. I would politely disagree and suggest that, rather than negative, it is an optimistically realistic mindset.

A mindset that encourages purposeful thinking and decision-making, taking charge of what we can, and identifying and potentially preventing (or at least minimizing) unwanted outcomes.

Thriving Not Just Surviving

Thriving not just surviving in Retirement is the goal! Achieving individual, relational, and family well-being while enjoying the highest quality of life possible is the desired outcome. So, what does it take to thrive?

Each of us are unique individuals with our own genetics, brain chemistry, temperament, personality, motivations and life experience. We do though have many things in common, not the least of which is the ability to decide to change. It is a characteristic that sets us humans apart from the other animals on this planet.

As smart as I think my dog and cat are, they do not have the capacity to wake up one morning, decide that their loud barking or middle of the night meowing is problematic, make a conscious choice to change, and create and implement a plan to fix it. They bark or meow from instinct and can be "trained" (hopefully) externally to behave differently. We however can create this process internally. It truly is a wonderful, though sometimes difficult to accomplish, aspect of the human experience. If change was easy everyone would "just do it" as the Nike commercials say. I don't know about you but my experience, personally and professionally, is that change can be challenging and at times scary. I have no doubt though it is possible!

I have observed that oftentimes we would rather see ourselves as victims of circumstance, blaming others, and cursing the world as it exists. The result is that we stay "stuck" in the situation.

I have found that a more productive approach involves taking charge of our situation and draw upon our skills, experiences, strengths and creativity, to redefine ourselves and move forward into the next "chapter" of our lives. I am not suggesting you take responsibility for things you can't control rather changing what you can, accept what you can't, and finding the wisdom to know the difference.

Change

How do we change? How do we make the most of the situations we encounter throughout our lifetime? Specifically, how, when and why do you change? Please take a moment and contemplate these questions. What motivates you to change something? How and when do you decide that you are ready, willing and able to make a shift? Understanding what helps you to decide or feel compelled to do things differently is quite important and personal. For what I might find motivating and encouraging you might find un-helpful, even irritating or off putting.

Interestingly our readiness to change actually has Stages developed by Prochaska and DiClemente[1] with specific strategies related to each stage, to assist in moving forward toward the end goal (whatever that might be). Think of changing as a continuum starting with:

- Pre-Contemplation: Not aware of the need to change and often un-willing or unable to recognize concerning or problematic behavior, even when it is brought to our attention.

- Contemplation: Able to acknowledge that perhaps something needs to change, especially after a "crisis". Not completely convinced and we often vacillate between, yes, it is a problem and then no, not so much.

- Preparation: Accepts need for change and begins to plan how and when to make it happen.

- Action: Moves forward doing things differently and behaving in new ways. Learns additional skills and strategies to challenge old ways of doing things and enhance quality of life.

- Maintenance: Changing and staying changed over time requires different strategies and skills to continue to think, act and feel in newly learned ways. And carry them forward.

As I mentioned before there are different strategies needed to be successful at each stage. Fortunately, we can learn the skills necessary to enhance our motivation, think and act differently and truly make lasting changes. It's also important to recognize that what may have worked well for us or motivated us at other times in our lives, may not work as well today or tomorrow. This probably is true at all stages of our journey through time as it is likely that we have had to assess, adjust and make new plans/changes, at other moments.

Change in Retirement

What makes Retirement so different or even unique? This is not just a rhetorical question. Rather it is one I hope you will ask yourself, your spouse/partner if relevant, and family members and friends; preferably sooner than later, ideally in your Pre-Retirement planning stage. Make sure that you revisit this question and answer at different phases and times in Retirement and adjust as necessary.

Healthy aging involves redefining ourselves, our relationships, expectations, needs, wants and priorities. While we need to accept these inevitable changes, it is important to realize many of them can be influenced but not controlled, managed but not avoided thus strengthening our capacity for resilience. This allows us to view retirement as an ongoing journey not a specific event or destination.

Resilience

The really good news is that there are things we can all do to increase our ability to respond to life in more resilient ways. Resiliency is not something that we either have or don't have. It's a trait or characteristic that can be developed. Resilience consists of a set of skills, beliefs and attitudes that enables us to perceive and respond to events and experiences in a way that we can handle and perhaps even grow.

What exactly is resiliency and why and how is it important? Psychological resilience is defined in the dictionary as an individual's ability to properly adapt to stress and adversity. We all know that stress and adversity can come in many shapes and sizes.

Some examples are family or relationship problems, health concerns, financial worries, or loss of a person, pet, or independence, just to mention a few. In other words, resilience is one's ability to bounce back from a negative experience.

According to *Psychology Today*, resilience[2] is an ineffable quality that allows some people to be knocked down by life and come back stronger than ever. Rather than letting failure overcome them and drain their resolve, they find a way to rise from the ashes. Simply put, it's one's ability to adapt to stressful situations or crises. More resilient people are better able to "roll with the punches"

Building Resilience

So, what are some ways that you can increase your resiliency and roll with challenging or difficult events rather than be knocked down or out by what comes our way? For additional information and suggestions, I recommend a Brochure entitled "The Road to Resilience" produced by the American Psychological Association (APA).[3]

There are though some practical things you can do. Engage in more of what you enjoy, be open to new experiences, people and learnings, choose flexibility over rigidity, frequently breathe deeply, remind yourself of what is going well and what you can be grateful for, nurture your relationships and identify and challenge negative beliefs and ways of thinking. Lastly, allow yourself to dream and imagine the Retirement you want to create and go for it!

Negative Patterns

We all have beliefs and views about the world and how things "should be." They are a result of our values, life experience, what we have been were taught and told by important people through-out our lives and expectations we hold, to mention a few variables.

Many of your beliefs and patterns of thinking may be healthy and positive adding to your overall health and resiliency. Some may be old and un-useful encouraging a "glass half full mindset" resulting in upset, anger and the perception that there is nothing you can do to influence your daily experiences and interactions.

Clients will say to me that's just the way I am and there's nothing I can do about it. Truly this is a learned belief and is not accurate. As was discussed earlier we can change and to be happy we must challenge such learning and replace it with a more useful perspective. Situations may not be what we would prefer, but often we view them as awful, terrible or unbearable, rather than unpleasant, but manageable.

I am not suggesting that you not feel what you feel or accept unacceptable behavior. Rather, I am encouraging you to view the situations through a different lens and put it in a different frame. Telling yourself that you can't stand what's occurring, it's horrible and should not be happening is debilitating, narrows the options and leaves little that can be done. Someone pulling out in front of you, cutting you off or other inappropriate action can be irritating, frustrating, upsetting and certainly is less than helpful, but it is not a terrible event that warrants in a rise in your blood pressure/heart rate, internal or external outrage (or road rage), leaving you, and often those around you in a negative and unhealthy place.

There are words that are "red flags" of such unhealthy beliefs and thoughts. They are should, shouldn't, must, have to and can't and they actually reflect a somewhat irrational method of processing. I encourage each of you to pay attention to how frequently you and others use these words/phrases and how immobilizing and intensely upsetting the outcomes are.

Try replacing the words above with I would prefer, I choose to or choose not to and other statements that are not so absolute.

Feelings

By their nature, emotions are consuming. In the moment, it is easy to simply remain inside them and not quite recognize that they are occurring. It is as though we're asleep, or helpless to act differently than the emotion wants you to act. We also often define some emotions as negative or bad, yet it is important to identify and express a wide range of emotions, not just the ones we perceive as positive or good. Different emotions have unique roles and purposes and within healthy boundaries and time frames they are necessary and useful. Emotions assist us in taking necessary steps to better care for ourselves and or others. They can indicate that something needs to be addressed or adjusted. Perhaps even that we need outside support and expertise such seeing as a Retirement Coach or a Counselor.

So, what are "normal" emotions that we label as "bad" and appropriate responses? How would one know if there is reason for concern? Let's explore a few very common ones:

- Anxiety: uncertainty, unknown worry, even momentary panic.

- Depression: feeling alone, disconnected, lack of daily connection. Can lead to loneliness and isolation.

- Perfectionism: overwhelming need to control outcomes and anything less than optimal is unacceptable.

- Alcohol, drug, and gambling misuse/abuse: engaging in any of these behaviors in increasing frequency, intensity or duration and continuing behavior with known/likely negative outcomes.

- Hoarding: Older adults often hang on to a lot more stuff than they need and insist on living in extremely cluttered potentially hazardous spaces; proven link to depression and need for control and often linked to unresolved previous losses.

- Loneliness and Isolation: considered a current health crisis, the new smoking, it can reduce life expectancy by 8 years, has a big negative effect on quality of life, and is the single largest predictor of dissatisfaction with health care, Mortality rate is greater than obesity. Estimated that loneliness and isolation results in $6.7 billion of additional Medicare spending annually.

- Grief and Mourning: healthy reaction to loss; duration is individual. We live in a culture that minimizes the importance of expressing grief and loss, often resulting in "complicated grief," keeping people "stuck" and unable to move forward.

Perhaps you are familiar with Dr. Elizabeth Kübler-Ross.[4] She was a physician pioneer specializing in working with patients, especially children, who were grappling with potentially terminal illnesses. She revolutionized our understanding and acceptance as to the importance of the process of mourning losses and created distinct stages of grieving. The Stages of Grief are Shock, Denial, Anger, Bargaining, Depression, Testing, and Acceptance. I include them here to normalize how necessary and healthy it is to allow ourselves the opportunity to acknowledge and mourn losses. Honestly, they relate to all of us, regardless of age or stage of life and it is my sincere hope to encourage all of us to grieve. In my experience ignoring or short-circuiting the process delays healing and at times results in becoming immobilized or stuck, which complicates and prolongs the hurt and pain.

Hopefully you have found the information and ideas presented in this chapter useful or at least interesting and worthy of consideration and even implementation! With all we are learning about the brain we know that it is important to challenge old beliefs about ageing and replace them with current understanding about how resiliency related skills, strategies and attitudes can, and do, impact our experience and longevity through-out the life span.

Mindfully choosing to focus on your physical, emotional and spiritual health and engaging in wellness related thoughts and actions, you can "live long and prosper" to quote a famous line from Star Trek. It is my sincere wish that each of us feel encouraged to stay active, find purpose, meaningful connections and activities, to seek out light, love and laughter and to continue to evolve into our very best selves possible.

Lastly, I hope you feel inspired to find fun, adventure, fellowship and positive intentions in your daily experiences and to make the years in

Retirement enjoyable. Bounce back from low points, challenge the negatives, hang onto the positive and allow yourself to makes your dreams come true. Perhaps the best is yet to come.

About Laura Riddle

Laura Riddle's passion is assisting Couples and Individuals to create their own personalized Retirement Revolution. Three out of four Boomers hate the word Retirement, hence the Revolution defined as "an uprising, overthrow, in favor of a new system or paradigm." Retirement today is active, engaged and connected; full of opportunities. Her focus is on the non-financial aspects of this amazing next phase of LIFE, assisting in the planning for and enjoying a happy, healthy and fulfilling Retirement experience.

Laura is a Certified Retirement Coach and Licensed Marriage and Family Therapist providing Coaching, Counseling, & Training for over 40 years. Her website is www.lriddlecoachcounselor.com

Notes

1. Prochaska J, DiClemente C. Towards a comprehensive model of change. In: Miller WR, Heather N, editors. Treating addictive behaviours: processes of change. New York: Pergamon, 1986. Search PubMed

2. "Resilience," *Psychology Today*, https://www.psychologytoday.com/us/basics/resilience.

3. "The Road to Resilience," *APA: Monitor on Psychology*, http://www.apa.org/helpcenter/roadresilience.aspx.

4. Elisabeth Kübler-Ross, *On Death and Dying* (New York: MacMillan, 1969.

Navigating Change Successfully In Your Season of Retirement

By Dale Chanaiwa

When you started planning for retirement, what was your primary focus? Was it:

- How much or how little can I contribute to my 401K, Roth IRA, Company Sponsored Pension Plan?

- When should I start my contributions?

- Do I understand the difference between these various methods of investing for retirement and which works best for me?

To justify delaying making contributions, did you tell yourself:

- "I'm still young! I have plenty of time."

- "I need every spare dime to put towards the purchase of my first home, a new car, or my dream vacation this year."

- "I can put off saving and investing in my retirement for another quarter, year or decade."

- "I can catch up later."

Or perhaps you are in total denial and believe you can make it on Social Security, alone. Besides, if push comes to shove, "I can always get me a part-time job to supplement my Social Security check, right?"

I know these are some of the things I told myself in the years leading up to the magical, yet somewhat fluid year of retirement.

Do you find yourself living on change figuratively and/or literally? No matter how well you did or did not focus on your finances, you find you did not focus as well as you could have on the other changes you would encounter in your season of retirement that impact you physically, mentally, socially, and spiritually.

Change is all around us. Nothing remains the same. We are either growing or deteriorating. Change can be like a roller coaster ride — full of sudden, unpredictable moves beyond your control. Some people love roller coaster rides and find them thrilling and exciting. Still, others fear them and want no part of them.

Change can be slow and minuscule, but even the slightest growth or deterioration can have a cumulative effect overtime. The results can be positive or negative in nature. For example, when it comes to financially planning for your retirement, small but consistent contributions to fund whatever method you select can result in tens of thousands, if not hundreds of thousands of dollars over the course of your work life.

Staying as physically active as possible can slow deterioration of muscles, joints and mental sharpness. Likewise, a decrease in physical activity can hasten their deterioration.

Slowly withdrawing from interactions or socialization with family, friends, colleagues and others can impact many aspects of your social, spiritual, physical, and mental well-being.

Like it or not, change is a choice. If you don't make the decision to change, someone else will make it for you. You can resist it, try to ignore it, or make up your mind to face it head on.

Whether you welcome, enjoy or avoid change at all costs, it is inevitable in every life season. If you want to navigate successfully the changes encountered in your season of retirement, you will need to be proactive, positive, and purposeful.

Be Proactive By Acknowledging, Assessing, Anticipating, Acting, And Adjusting

Start by acknowledging change is inevitable. Burying your head in the sand will not stop change. Pay attention to the signs and warnings of impending change. Whether the change is favorable or unfavorable it will require you to make some adjustments.

Assessing where you stand is crucial. Take inventory of where you are not only financially, but spiritually, mentally, physically, and socially.

If you plan to continue to work, make sure the decision-makers know your strengths and abilities.

This will be crucial if your organization is considering cutbacks or restructuring. Make sure management has a current resume on file which also highlights your goals and interests. If cutbacks are a possibility, you don't want the decision-makers wondering whether you are expendable or an invaluable asset they should hang on to.

Be sure you assess the organization or team, as well. Do you really want to remain a part of it? Is it time for you to explore other opportunities and move on? Or do you make the decision that you have had a great career, but it is now time to focus more on the life side of work/life balance that you have been juggling for so long?

Are you the best you can be when it comes to your physical and mental well-being? Working provides income for you and your family. However, it also requires you to keep physically active and interact with others. It gives you a reason to get up and get going each morning. If you are no longer working:

- What is your reason for getting up each day?

- What will you do with your time?

- Will you become the proverbial couch potato?

- Or will you find new or renewed interests that get you out of the house, moving and interacting with others?

Perhaps you want to focus on volunteering and giving back to the community at large. Volunteering will help to keep you physically strong and mentally sharp. It is a great way to fulfill your spiritual needs and beliefs, also.

No matter what, you must assess your needs, desires, and purpose for the season, whether a current or future season.

Anticipating that the rules will change should be a given. And they will change often. Make sure you know and understand them. They will have a far-reaching impact on your ability to function on all levels.

Change will challenge you, but challenges help you to grow. Therefore, remain positive. Negativity makes it difficult to navigate change. That is why I strive to remind myself of another one of my Diamond Dale Discoveries (personal "a-ha" moments): "I may not be able to control the challenges life throws at me today. However, I can control the attitude I throw back. Therefore, maintain an attitude of gratitude!"

Finally, acting by developing, implementing, and adjusting, when needed, a purposeful plan of action to navigate change head on is a must.

If you plan to continue to work, your plan should include strategies to make sure you remain marketable. Take advantage of any training offered and paid for by your employer. If there is external training that is key to your marketability, make sure you get it even if you must pay for it yourself. Invest in *you* not only financially, but also physically, mentally, spiritually and socially. You are worth it! You deserve it!

Bottom line: change is a choice. Don't be fooled. No decision is a decision. If you fail to make a needed decision or choose your path by default, someone else may end up making it for you. And I guarantee, you will not always be happy with the choices others make for you.

No matter what, take the time to make yourself the priority. After all, it is your time, your talent, your treasures, your season!

About The Author

Known as an encourager and facilitator, Dr. Dale Chanaiwa is a motivational speaker, life coach, retirement coach, mentor, and published author. She has a doctorate degree in law and more than 40 years of knowledge and expertise in the healthcare and business development industries. She has created multiple programs designed to empower women to enhance their added-value. Your added-value is comprised of your gifts, talents, expertise, education, and life experiences that make you a unique individual, destined to do what you have been called to do. For additional information regarding programs and services offered, please visit her website, www.seasonedsassysisterhood.com, or email her at seasonedsassysister@gmail.com.

Before You Retire: Tips for Your Transition and Topics to Explore with Your HR Department

By Michele Fannt-Harris

American Express advertises "Don't leave home without it." I say, "Don't retire from your job without first talking to your Human Resources office. HR professionals have a wealth of information to help employees about the benefits your company offers both *while* you are working and after you retire. HR can set your retirement on a prosperous path. It's time to get your portfolio, health care and other financial benefits in order so you can enjoy the next stage of your life.

Here are some retirement issues you should discuss with your human resources office:

Social Security

As long as you continue to work, you and your employer are paying Social Security and Medicare taxes. You are entitled to a retirement benefit from Social Security if you are fully insured and are at least 62 years of age. Full retirement age for Social Security benefits is 66. If you retire at age 62, your benefit will be permanently reduced. If you work past full retirement age, you can collect Social Security benefits but there is a limit on how much you can earn without penalty to your Social Security benefit. If you choose not to receive benefits at full retirement age, you will receive special credits for delaying your retirement until you reach age 70.

Life Insurance

Many employers provide life insurance benefits to employees as part of their benefit package. As an employee you don't pay out of pocket for these benefits, but life insurance and disability insurance coverage is likely to end on your last day of employment.

Review your employer group plan to see if you have the option for conversion or portability. Some group employer insurance plans allow terminating employees the ability to continue coverage for all or a portion of the same coverage without submitting evidence of good health. So, check your current life insurance and disability plans to find the specific options that are available to you.

A life insurance conversion option gives you the opportunity to obtain an individual life insurance policy that accumulates cash value and is offered at individual insurance rates. The two types of conversion life insurance policies that are offered include whole life insurance or universal life insurance:

- *Whole life insurance* may be kept for a person's entire life and pays a benefit upon death. Premiums are fixed throughout the life of the policy. The premiums for whole life policies are higher than premiums for term insurance because whole life policies build cash value that can be treated as an asset (for example, they can support loans). In addition,

341

they include a cash surrender value. This means that if you surrender the policy, you can receive cash or continue your coverage without further premium payments. Your amount of continued coverage would be based on your cash surrender value.

- *Universal life insurance* combines the low-cost protection of term insurance with a savings feature. Premiums are put into an account that is invested. Each month, the cost of insurance is deducted from the account. The account builds cash value from which you can take loans and provides flexibility in premium payment.

On the other hand, portability of your employer-sponsored life insurance often provides continuation of low-cost term life insurance. Your premiums may be lower; however, no cash value is accumulated, and you cannot use this as a basis for loans nor can you receive a cash refund if you surrender the policy.

Whether you choose to continue your term life insurance policy or convert to whole life insurance or universal life insurance, most insurance companies require that you submit your completed application within one month after your insurance policy ends. Having the talk with your human resources professional before you leave your position will help you to make the right choice for your life insurance.

Disability Insurance

Most employer-sponsored disability insurance plans end on your last day of employment. Long-term disability insurance is usually not available for conversion for retirees. You are encouraged to seek disability insurance on your own prior to retirement.

Health Insurance

Most employer-sponsored health insurance plans are paid on a monthly basis, so if you resign any time during the month, your health insurance is covered through the end of the month. Just be aware that if you resign on the 30th of the month, you very likely will begin your retirement with no health insurance benefit "window."

Before you retire, ask your HR professional when your health insurance plan might end under different scenarios. You are eligible for Medicare Plan A (hospital insurance) and Part B (medical insurance) at age 65, whether you are working or retired. Your spouse, at age 65, is also eligible. If you are still working at age 65 and are under your employer-sponsored health plan, Medicare becomes your secondary health insurance payer. If you reject the employer plan, Medicare will be the primary health insurance payer.

Medicare Plan A and B do not cover copayments, coinsurance, deductibles and medical insurance coverage outside of the United States. Consider purchasing a Medigap policy, which will pay the health care costs not covered by Parts A and B. You

343

can purchase Medigap insurance through a private insurance company. You will pay a monthly premium for the Medigap policy in addition to your Part B monthly premium.

Prescription drug benefits are available under Medicare Part D. This coverage, run by Medicare-approved private insurance companies, helps cover the costs of prescription drugs. Prescription drug coverage is voluntary.

Medicare offers prescription drug coverage to all individuals covered by Medicare. To get prescription drug coverage, you must have Medicare Part A or Part B and you must join a prescription drug plan run by an insurance company or other private company approved by Medicare. If you do not elect to join a Medicare prescription drug plan when you are first eligible, and you do not have other prescription drug coverage, you will likely pay a late enrollment penalty if you later elect coverage. Even if you don't plan to receive your monthly Social Security benefits when you are age 65, be sure to register for Medicare three months before turning age 65. If you do not sign up for Medicare Part B when you are first eligible, your coverage may be delayed and you may be required to pay a late enrollment penalty.

COBRA

If you can't decide which health insurance plan to keep when you retire prior to age 65, consider keeping your employer-sponsored health plan through COBRA (The Consolidated Omnibus

Budget Reconciliation Act.) This federal law requires that most group health plans offer employees and their families the opportunity to continue their health care coverage after job loss or other "qualifying event" (e.g., voluntary termination, that would result in a loss of coverage under the group health insurance plan). You are eligible to continue your group health insurance for up to 18 months. You have 60 days from your termination date to consider accepting COBRA. The first premium payment can be charged as early as 45 days after the beginning of coverage. You are allowed a 30 day grace period if you fail to pay your premiums on time. After that, your COBRA insurance can be terminated.

In an ideal situation, you should begin your search for alternative health insurance within approximately one year from accepting COBRA. Because the maximum coverage period for COBRA is 18 months, give yourself plenty of time to find a health plan that is right for you and your dependents.

401(k) and Retirement Plans

Don't forget to ask your Human Resources professional about the withdrawal rules for your company's 401(k) plan. The Plan Sponsor Council of America says that two-thirds of large 401(k) plans allow retired participants to withdraw money in regularly scheduled installments — monthly or quarterly. Other plans allow retirees to take partial withdrawals whenever they want.

Distributions taken from the traditional 401(k) are subject to your current ordinary income tax rate at the time of withdrawal. If you have a Roth account, you have already paid income taxes on your contributions, so your withdrawals are not subject to further taxation.

You are not required to take distributions from your account as soon as you retire. As long as you have at least $5,000 invested in the 401(k), you can let the account continue to earn dividends and maintain itself. Once you retire, you cannot contribute to a 401(k) held by a previous employer. If your 401(k) has less than $5,000 at retirement, a lump-sum distribution will be generated by your plan administrator.

You must begin to take the required minimum distribution from your 401(k) account by April 1 following the year you turn 70½. Some plans may allow you to defer distributions until the year you retire if you retire after age 70½. Once you are required to take your required minimum distributions, you must take regular, periodic distributions, which are calculated on your life expectancy and your account balance. You may withdraw more than the minimum required distribution, but you cannot withdraw less.

If you retire and wish to continue contributing funds to your 401(k) account, you can elect to roll your account into an IRA. You can contribute to a Roth IRA for as long as you like, but you must stop contributions to a traditional IRA after age 70½.

Does your employer contribute or match your employee contributions? If so, when does the employer match occur? Some employers match the employee contributions every pay period or at the end of the month, while other employers have a profit-sharing program that only provides a contribution at the end of the year. Check your retirement plan to see when employer contributions are made. If you are able, you can time your retirement date to maximize retirement contributions from your employer.

Supplemental Benefits

Do you have supplemental benefits through your employer? Usually, you pay the monthly premium for supplemental benefits through payroll deduction but receive a group discount because your employer guarantees payment to the benefits carrier. Supplemental benefits may include home and auto insurance, AFLAC, gym membership, supplemental life and disability insurance, pet insurance, etc. Remember to ask your Human Resources professional about continuing these benefits after retirement. You may have to contact each benefits carrier directly.

Although you may lose your employer group discount, you may receive a similar discount for similar benefits through group memberships, such as AARP or your college alumni association.

Long-Term Care Insurance

Long-Term Care insurance helps you cover costs associated with a chronic illness or disability. Unfortunately, fewer employers are offering this benefit. If you are fortunate to have this benefit through your employer, please be sure to take this benefit with you upon retirement. Check with your HR department to see whether the long-term care insurance policy is portable or can be converted to an individual policy. The number of insurance companies that provide long-term care is decreasing, so this is definitely a good benefit to keep!

Vacation or PTO Leave

Does your employer allow you to accrue vacation or PTO (paid time off) leave? If so, you need to plan your retirement at a time that will give you the most vacation leave or PTO leave accrual. This benefit can provide a significant financial boost to help support you as you leave the world of steady pay checks.

Employer Benefits

Does your organization offer special benefits to retirees or other benefits you can retain after retirement? For example, one benefit that National Cooperative Bank, NA, offers its employees and retirees is consumer banking services.

Employees can earn an extra one percent of interest on savings accounts and certificates of deposit.

Employees can continue this service after retirement under some conditions related to age and years of service. The extended additional interest on savings accounts allows retiring employees to continue to increase their retirement savings and feel that they are still a part of the NCB family. This type of benefit is extremely helpful in today's economy, when the average savings account pays less than 1% interest.

Outplacement Services and Career Coaching

Were you forced into retirement due to a reduction-in-force (RIF)? Did your employer offer outplacement services or career development seminars to people like you who were affected? If so, it's wise to take advantage of the outplacement and career coaching services. Even if you don't plan to return to full-time employment, these career services can help you define the next chapter in your life.

One of the benefits of working with outplacement counselors or career coaches is they provide in-depth self-assessments to help you define your personal motivators and your values. Career coaches maintain an open mind and help you think outside of the "normal" retirement box. They will help you strategize and create a retirement path that is unique to you. Baby Boomers today think differently than their parents' generation. Many mature workers consider alternative options — like serving on a board of directors, starting a business or volunteering their time — and a career coach can bridge the gap by focusing you on your applicable skills and personal values to guide you to your next venture.

Staying at Home and Turning Over a New Leaf

Some employers see the advantage of the mature worker who has knowledge of the company and its products and services. Ask your human resources office if there are other ways that you can serve the company after you retire.

You might serve as a brand ambassador for your former employer by representing the company at trade shows and conferences. As a brand ambassador, you are a seasoned professional who knows the company's product and service, so you can sell the company brand to new and existing clients.

You may not want to work regularly for the company, but would like to return for small projects. Let the human resources office know that you are available for temporary assignments after your retirement. You might take on a clerical assignment, such as filling in for the receptionist or preparing a bulk mail assignment. Retirees can also fill in for regular employees who are on FMLA leave, vacation or sabbaticals. Retirees get to return to the workplace and connect with former colleagues, as well as earn extra income without the pressures of a long-term commitment or project assignment.

If you decide to start your own consulting business when you retire, start with your current employer as your first client. Market yourself to your boss, other executives and the human resources office of your employer. Working as a consultant allows you to remain engaged in your career field and enter the world of entrepreneurship. It also does not allow you to be paid through payroll, so you will need to work with an attorney and an accountant to establish business accounts as a sole proprietor, but these are easy hurdles to navigate.

Whatever path you decide to take in your "new" retirement, don't begin your journey before you talk with the human resources office of your current employer. The HR office has a wealth of information that will be helpful to you as you plan the next chapter of your life.

About The Author

Michele Fantt Harris, is EVP, HR, for the National Cooperative Bank in Washington, D.C. A seasoned HR professional, this is Michele's sixth anthology. Her latest, *You@Work*, is available on Amazon. An Associate Certified Coach and a Certified Career Management Coach through The Academies, Inc., she serves on the Leadership Center for Excellence for the Board of Regents. Michele received her BA from the University of Maryland, Baltimore County, an MAS from Johns Hopkins, and a JD from the University of Baltimore. A certified senior HR expert, Michele teaches at Prince Georges Community College and Catholic University. Contact Michele at Michele.Harris19@gmail.com.

Notes

Boyte-White, Claire (2018 March 27). *How a 401(k) Works after Retirement.* Received from http://www.investopedia.com/articles/personal-fiance/111615/how-401k-works-after-retirement.asp.

Fantt Harris, M. et al (2018) "Transitioning into Retirement." *You@Work: Unlocking Human Potential in the Workplace.* (pp. 105-117). Kenosha, WI: Silver Tree Publishing.

Bureau of National Affairs. (2017). *Social Security & Medicare Fact Sheet:* Arlington, VA: Bureau of National Affairs.

Retirement 2030 And Beyond

By Robert Laura

Over 10 years ago, I started doing my first non-financial retirement workshops. I was excited to try something new and finally bring together my social work background and what I had learned about life in retirement. There was only one problem. Not everyone was ready for it.

In fact, it was a regular occurrence for people to actually get up and leave in the middle of my workshop. Despite marketing the program as completely non-financial, people still associated retirement as a financial event. So, when they figured out I wasn't going to be talking about asset allocation, diversification, or Social Security, they didn't think they needed to be there. It was very uncomfortable to say the least.

Fast forward a decade and you get a very different picture. Not only do more people attend and participate in non-financial retirement workshops, but there are more opportunities than ever to write, speak, and educate the public as it gains mainstream acceptance.

It's a welcomed change but leaves me wondering what the next 10-20 years may bring as the concept of retirement continues to evolve. Will retirement in 2030 or 2040 be vastly different than today, or will it share some of the same core characteristics. Here are several trends and concepts I expect to reshape the concept of retirement as we know it today.

Retirement Regrets Shift The Planning Focus

As people approach retirement, it's common for some to say, "I wish I would have started saving earlier." Many people still assume that money is the key aspect for making a successful transition from work life to home life, but ask someone who has plenty of money but is struggling with a health issue, is estranged from their children, or feels lonely in retirement, and you get a very different picture.

As retirement planning gets more personal, the things that people will regret not doing won't have anything to do with money. The focus will shift to health, relationships, and finding a career they truly loved. On the surface, it may not seem like an earth-shattering prediction for the next decade or two, but it will absolutely help transform the retirement planning process.

Over the last several years, it's been common for people in or near retirement to say that they regret not saving more or starting earlier, and younger workers, and employers have taken the message to heart. As a result, many new professionals are automatically enrolled into a retirement savings program as soon as they start their first job. This is great, but it's only part of the total equation and doesn't mean that if they stick to that they are going to be happy, healthy, or connected when they reach retirement age.

Therefore, as the message about what is truly important about life after work trickles down, new non-financial planning programs will emerge where coaches and counselors are given access to employees in the same way that local 401(k) consultants conduct seminars and one-on-one meetings. The only difference being that the focus will be on who they are and what they are doing outside of work.

This type of truly comprehensive retirement planning will take place at younger and younger ages instead of being reserved for those who are 5-10 years away from retirement or for those who are forced into it sooner than expected. Finally, having a balanced life where one can make an impact at work, home, and within their community will be on an equal value to having a balanced portfolio for retirement.

Sharing Economy Finally Reaches The Workplace

In the last few years, it's become increasingly common to see various types of sharing services. Whether it's a bike, car, or room, the next round of sharing will come from the workplace in terms of job-sharing.

The concept of job sharing isn't anything new. In fact, it's very common in some career spaces such as education where two different teachers, for example, will share a classroom. This allows them to devote specific time to their professional goals while giving them the flexibility to raise a family.

Similar to young teachers who have dual motivations, many people reach traditional retirement age and want to find a balance between their careers and other things they want to do such as travel, spending time with a new grandchild, or even starting their own business. They aren't ready to give up the things that work provides for them, but also want some flexibility to stop and smell the roses, if you will.

In order to accomplish this, I envision a modified version of an online dating where people can enter in everything from a DISC profile or other personality type, years of experience, education, skills, and motivations, along with a personal narrative in an effort to get matched with someone similar to them.

Whether it's for dedicated time off to help an aging parent, raise a grandchild, take a European river cruise, or recover from a hip or knee replacement, it will not only keep people in the workplace longer, but also improve work satisfaction and productivity.

The Haves And Have Nots Turn Into Watchers Versus Doers

No doubt that technology will play a more significant role in the future of retirement. In fact, I believe it will dramatically improve the quality of life in a number of ways:

- Easy access to doctors and treatments over the internet

- Drones delivering healthy foods and medications to keep people young

- 360-degree cameras combined with virtual reality glasses will allow retirees to avoid missing a grandchild's sporting events, give them virtual access to museums around the globe, and even learn a new language or pick up an instrument, all from the comfort of their own home.

- Driverless cars will keep people mobile for longer periods of time

- Clothing and home security sensors will not only monitor your heart-rate, but also watch what you are putting in and taking out of fridge

These are all very positive things that will likely add even more years to one's life expectancy. However, despite all of these advances, it will cause a shift between who is part of the Haves and Have Nots. As technology levels the playing field, the difference between these groups will become those who can only watch or see things versus those who actually do them in real life.

The Haves will once again put the benefits of staying mentally and physically active at the top of the retirement spectrum as they will have the capacity, strength and energy to do more in real life rather than succumbing to a virtual world of retirement. As a result, it will be common to ask, "Did you watch it, or do it?"

Fraud & Medial Kidnappings Escalate

On the scary side of things, our rapidly aging society will face some hurdles in terms of fraud and health care. To begin, as we move toward a paperless society, fraud will increase as use of technology eliminates cash methods of tracking it via ledgers and such.

In terms of health care, I expect to see an increase in medical kidnappings as people will begin to, more or less, traffic seniors, especially those who are in serious mental decline but otherwise healthy (Alzheimer's and Dementia)

The sad part is, as people seek to cut long-term care costs, they will need to send loved ones to private group homes that look good on the outside but do something very different on the inside. In particular, retirees who need expensive medication and who are receiving maximum social security and pension payments will be prime targets.

Imagine a group home taking in 10-12 seniors who have social security payments around $2,500 a month, plus a pension of $1,000 or more, plus require daily care and medications. It could amount to more than $35,000 in income, per month, not to mention reimbursements for Medicare and Medicaid for their care and medications.

Facilities will position themselves as guardians and essentially kidnap people by denying family members access to them and their treatments and using their financial resources at their own discretion. Many will be forced to live in unsanitary conditions, wander around without much direction or supervision, and become a constant source for news stories about senior fraud and abuse.

What may be even worse is that it won't just happen on a group scale. Expect more family fights for the right to take care of mom or dad, especially in situations where their retirement payments are healthy, but their mind is not

For example, one sibling will become guardian of mom or dad and deny other family members access to them and use their income and assets how they want. While conditions may not be as unsanitary as a group situation, nevertheless, it will likely mean a lower standard of care and costly legal battles to address the situation.

While these are just a handful of the many things that may come about as retirement continues to evolve, I also think there will be a growing place for Retirement Coaches — those special individuals who are teachers at heart, genuinely interested in people and what makes them tick, and have a deep desire to not only help people see and begin to plan for changes likes these, but also know how to help people thrive in this next phase of life.

The years 2030 and beyond may seem like they far away, but they will be here before you know it and along the way, it will put Retirement Coaching and make many of the authors in the book, permanent fixtures in the new era of retirement.

About The Author

Robert Laura is the founder of the Retirement Coaches Association and RetirementProject.org. He is the leading voice for the retirement coaching industry and has pioneered many tools and resources to help people prepare for the non-financial aspects of retirement including the Certified Professional Retirement Coach CRPC training and designation. He is the author of several books and guides including Naked Retirement and Retirement Rx. He is also a nationally syndicated columnist for Forbes.com and Financial Advisor Magazine. Robert is a sought after corporate trainer, speaker, consultant, and financial expert witness. He can be reached at rl@robertlaura.com

About The Retirement Coaches Association

The Retirement Coaches Association is a group of dedicated professionals who are committed to helping people thrive in this next phase of life! Our goal is to not only help you see and experience retirement in a truly different and more meaningful light but also to help you:

- ☑ Formulate your vision for your future.
- ☑ Unlock and expand your potential.
- ☑ Reinforce and maximize your strengths.
- ☑ Formulate a plan to keep you relevant, connected, and active.
- ☑ Provide encouragement and objective feedback.
- ☑ Develop balance in your life now and in the future.
- ☑ Support your efforts and provide you with increased confidence.
- ☑ Brainstorm strategies to accomplish your goals.
- ☑ Uncover and assist in developing your unique abilities.
- ☑ Inspire you toward continuous improvement and unparalleled results.

To find a coach near you or to learn more about the organization and our mission to change the focus of retirement planning, please visit:
http://retirementcoachesassociation.org

Made in the USA
Columbia, SC
21 August 2019